TLINGIT INDIANS
OF
ALASKA

9-25-08

To the English man
who wants to learn.

Enjoy

Wendy Speier-Trost

Alaska

The Rasmuson Library
Historical Translation Series
Volume II
Marvin W. Falk, Editor

Additional titles in the Series:

All titles listed are available from the University of Alaska Press.

TLINGIT INDIANS OF ALASKA

by Archimandrite Anatolii Kamenskii

Translated, with an Introduction and
Supplementary Material
by
Sergei Kan

The University of Alaska Press
Fairbanks

Translation of
Indiane Aliaski,
Odessa, 1906
International Standard Series Number: 0890-7935
International Standard Book Number: 0-912006-18-8
Library of Congress Catalog Card Number: 85-51786
English Translation © 1985 by the University of Alaska Press.

CONTENTS

ILLUSTRATIONS LIST

1. Archimandrite Anatolii (Kamenskii). From the *Russian Orthodox American Messenger*, vol. 7, no. 6, p 91.

2. St. Michael Brotherhood members in front of St. Michael's Cathedral, ca. 1900. E.W. Merrill Collection, Stratton Memorial Library, Sheldon Jackson College, Sitka, Alaska.

3,4. Kaagwaantaan Chief Tlanteech in European and traditional dress. E.W. Merrill Collection, Stratton Memorial Library, Sheldon Jackson College, Sitka, Alaska.

5. Jacob Kanagood, first President of the St. Michael Brotherhood wearing the brotherhood sash and badges. E.W. Merrill Collection, Stratton Memorial Library, Sheldon Jackson College, Sitka, Alaska.

6. Chief of the Angoon Deisheetaan clan Kichnal or Killisnoo Jake ca. 1900. Vince Soboleff Collection, Alaska Historical Library, Juneau.

7. A studio photograph of Native Sitka women. Case and Draper Photographers. Alaska Historical Library, Juneau.

8. Reproduced in Kamenskii's original with the title "a hundred year old woman who remembers Baranov." Vincent Soboleff Collection, Alaska Historical Library, Juneau.

9. Native policeman in Sitka ca. 1890. Edward De Groff, Photographer, Alaska Historical Library, Juneau.

ACKNOWLEDGEMENTS

I would like to acknowledge the help of several organizations and individuals that made this project possible. First and foremost, I wish to thank the National Endowment for the Humanities, an independent Federal agency, for the Translation Grant that supported my work in 1983-1984; additional financial assistance was provided by the Elmer E. Rasmuson Library of the University of Alaska, Fairbanks through the kind efforts of Dr. Marvin Falk, Curator of Rare Books. Lydia Black, Jeff Leer, Richard Pierce, Richard and Nora Dauenhauer, Michael Krauss, Marilyn Knapp, Robert N. DeArmond, Peter Corey, and Isabel Miller offered valuable advice on ethnographic, linguistic, historical, and biographical matters. Two people whose help has been of utmost significance deserve a special word of appreciation. They are Alexander S. Kan, my father, whose tireless efforts and professional expertise produced vital bibliographic references available only in Soviet libraries, and Mark Jacobs, Jr., Second Vice President of the Central Council of the Tlingit and Haida Indian Tribes of Alaska, who read the *Tlingit Indians of Alaska* and made extensive comments on it. Members of the staff of the Manuscript Division of the Library of Congress, the Alaska State Historical Library in Juneau, and the Stratton Memorial Library of the Sheldon Jackson College in Sitka were also extremely helpful. Finally, I would like to thank Nancy W. Glover and the staff of the Microform Reading Rooms of the Hatcher Library of the University of Michigan for assistance in obtaining and reviewing microfilms needed for the completion of this project.

Fr. Anatolii Kamenskii
TLINGIT INDIANS OF ALASKA
TRANSLATOR'S INTRODUCTION

The present work is an annotated translation of materials containing information on the history and culture of the Tlingit Indians of southeastern Alaska written by Russian Orthodox missionaries at the end of the nineteenth and the beginning of the twentieth centuries. The major text among them is a monograph by Fr. Anatolii Kamenskii entitled *Tlingit Indians of Alaska*,[1] published in Russia in 1906. Other sources were found in the *Russian Orthodox American Messenger*, an Orthodox periodical published in New York since 1896, in the Alaska Church Collection of the Manuscript Division of the Library of Congress, and in the Alaska State Historical Library of Juneau, Alaska.

Written by a Sitka parish priest who spent three years laboring among the Tlingit, *Tlingit Indians of Alaska*, combined with other documents presented here, constitutes a valuable source of data for the study of the Tlingit culture, society, and history of the turn of the century, the activity of the Russian missionaries in southeastern Alaska after 1867, and the general history of the Territory of Alaska under the American administration.

In the last decades, the significance of the ethnographic and historical data on the Alaskan natives provided by the writings of the Russian missionaries has been recognized by Western scholars. This has been reflected in a recent publication of several annotated translations of books, diaries, journals, and letters by Orthodox clergymen who worked in Alaska from the end of the eighteenth century (e.g., Black 1977; Pierce 1978, 1980). Because of the language barrier and difficulties of access, most of the Russian materials pertaining to the Tlingit remained outside the scope of the American anthropological research of the twentieth century (Swanton 1908, 1909; Oberg 1937; Olson 1967; de Laguna 1960, 1972). *Tlingit Indians of Alaska* serves as an important link between these studies and the earlier works by such Russian writers as Bishop Innokentii Veniaminov (St. Innocent), Lisianskii, Litke, Khlebnikov and others. Unlike the classical study of Tlingit culture by Veniaminov (1840), which has been extensively quoted by such Western scholars as Holmberg (1856) and Krause (1885), and has been translated into English,[2] Kamenskii's work remains unknown outside the USSR. Several Soviet scholars have used its information (Averkieva 1960; Meletinskii 1979) and have emphasized its importance.[3] The present translation is based on a xerographic copy of the book received from the Lenin Library of Moscow, USSR.

Articles on the same subject published in the *Russian Orthodox American Messenger* and especially archival documents from the Alaska Church Collection translated here have also been largely neglected by historians and anthropologists, with the exception of B. Smith's (1980) historical research on the Orthodox Church in Alaska, and several studies of native Alaskan cultures that have used translated selections from the Alaska Church Collection published in the *Documents Relative to the History of Alaska* (1936-1938) (e.g., VanStone 1967; Townsend 1981). The value of these materials is increased when other written sources, e.g., U.S. government documents, newspaper reports, Presbyterian publications, and so forth, are used to verify and cross-check their information. In the work on this translation, I have tried to do precisely that, and have also consulted enthographic data I obtained in southeastern Alaska from Tlingit consultants during the 1979-1980 fieldwork season. Having a native perspective on the events and phenomena described by the missionaries has been crucial for correcting some of their biases and providing a more rounded picture of the complex issues they discussed.

The translation is accompanied by an annotation, with references to relevant ethnographic and historical studies, corrections and clarifications of the data presented, and other comments. In addition, it contains a glossary of geographical terms, personal names, Tlingit and Russian terms, as well as a subject index and a bibliography.

The remaining portion of this introduction presents a biography of Fr. Anatolii Kamenskii and an evaluation of his work as a missionary and an ethnographer.

Information on Kamenskii's life is quite limited, with major sources being his own writings, documents from the Alaska Church Collection, and an article that appeared in the *Russian Orthodox American Messenger* in connection with his departure from the United States in 1903.[4] Born into a clergyman's family in the 1860s, he graduated from the Samara Seminary in 1886. Upon graduation, he became the inspector of that seminary, and in 1888 was ordained as a priest in a rural parish of the Samara Province. Kamenskii had been married for nine years, became a widower, and entered the St. Petersburg Theological Academy in the early 1890s. He graduated in 1895 as a candidate, which meant that he had spent three years there, had high grades, and wrote a satisfactory dissertation, but did not defend it to become a master or a doctor. Theological academies were the highest institutions in the educational system of the Russian Church (see Freeze 1983). Their aim was to train future church scholars, who became teachers in seminaries and academies, as well as the "learned monks" of the ecclesiastical hierarchy who became archimandrites, rectors and bishops. Fr. Anatolii must have taken his monastic vows soon after graduation, since he was referred to as a "hiermonk" as early as in 1895. In the academy, he was trained in various theological disciplines as well as history, history of religion, "polemical theology" aimed at criticizing non-Orthodox Christian denominations, and a number of other subjects. The focus of such education was on independent student compositions and theses. In addition, some academies included courses on science, medicine and agronomy in their curricula. Kamenskii never became an outstanding scholar of the stature of Bishop Innokentii Veniaminov (St. Innocent), but his considerable erudition was reflected in his ethnographic writings.

Politically, like many of the Orthodox clergymen of his era, Kamenskii was rather conservative, which is suggested by his lectures delivered in one of Odessa's high schools [*gimnazia*] in 1904-1907.[5] Above all, he was a Russian patriot and nationalist, who firmly believed that the Orthodox religion and the monarchic system of government were far superior to those of other European countries and the United States. He missed his mother country while serving in Alaska and Minnesota, and frequently asked to be sent back. He did not think that a "true Russian" would voluntarily remain in Alaska after its sale to the U.S., and claimed that all who remained there after 1867 were Jews, Finns, or persons of mixed Russian-native background. He despised the Russian immigrant press for its attacks on the Empire and had a negative view of Polish and Ukrainian nationalism. To his mind, Orthodoxy was the main force in maintaining Slavic identity among Eastern European immigrants in the United States. At the same time, he was fascinated by America, its industrial achievements, and vibrant political and social life.

He arrived in Sitka, Alaska, in 1895 to become its parish priest and the dean of clergy [*blagochinnyi*] of the Sitka District of the Alaska Diocese. In Sitka the young missionary was immediately confronted with a variety of difficult tasks and complicated issues. He had to serve two types of parishioners, with different cultural backgrounds and needs. On the one hand, there were some Russians and a larger group of the so-called Creoles, persons of mixed Russian-native descent. While some Russian and a few Creole families were well-to-do or at least maintained a decent lifestyle, a large number of them were poor, often unemployed, and many engaged in drinking, prostitution, and petty crime. In the social hierarchy of Sitka, they occupied an intermediate position between the "white" Americans and the Tlingit Indians. While some Russian-Creole families had ties with the Tlingit through the institution of godparenthood and joint participation in the Orthodox Church, some of them resented being considered only slightly above the Indians by the town's American population.

Fr. Anatolii was appalled by the social and moral condition of many of his parishioners, as well as by the lack of dedication to the Church and to the Russian culture among the younger, American-born Creoles. In his reports to the Bishop of Alaska, Nikolai (Ziorov), he complained that the younger generation had acquired a taste for the American "freedom," and no longer obeyed the priest or attended the church services regularly. As an educator and a Russian patriot, he was particularly disappointed that "most Russian and Creole children are totally ignorant about Orthodoxy, do not know a single prayer, have an indifferent attitude to the Church, and some of them can barely speak the Russian language" (Report to Bishop Nikolai, April 1896, ACC, D-432).[6]

As the inspector of the local Orthodox educational institutions, Kamenskii revived a parish school for the Russian and Creole children (where he was one of the teachers), with an emphasis on teaching Russian, as well as the Orthodox dogma, church singing, arithmetic, geography, history, and English. Under his direction, a new building was erected for the orphanage that admitted Russian, Creole, and native children and was aimed at training workers for the Alaskan mission—psalm-readers, teachers, deacons, etc. In addition to standard religious and secular subjects, this school taught Tlingit, Aleut, and other native Alaskan languages. Among its graduates were several Tlingit men who became religious instructors, interpreters, and lay leaders in later years (e.g., Paul Liberty, Eli Katanook, Innocent Williams, etc.). Fr. Anatolii's educational efforts also included developing new statutes for the orphanages and grade schools of Alaska (*Russian Orthodox American Messenger,* 1897, vol. 3, no. 3).

To upgrade the morality of the adult members of his church, Kamenskii revived a Russian Society of St. Nicholas, whose major aims were promoting temperance, mutual aid, peace, and preservation of the Russian language and culture among parish members. His efforts were only partially successful; part of the Russian-Creole population continued to experience some of the same social and economic problems as before, while many of its younger members were gradually assimilated into the local American society through intermarriage, joining other churches, and changing their names. His attempts to preserve the Russian language among the younger generation could not stop the tide of Americanization, in that era when being American was more desirable than remaining Russian.

Despite his concern with the Russian-Creole parishioners, Kamenskii's major efforts were aimed at working with the growing Tlingit membership of the Orthodox Church. Here the state of affairs was more encouraging. After a period of decline caused by the sale of Alaska and the reduction of the financial aid and manpower, the Russian Church increased its missionary efforts in southeastern Alaska in the mid-1880s. In the era of the nationalist government of Alexander III and the Procurator of the Holy Synod Pobedonostsev, the

Alaska mission began to receive more money and was able to recruit additional clergymen. More importantly, this was the period when the Tlingit of Sitka and several neighboring villages began asking for baptism and showing signs of interest in the Russian Church. It should be pointed out that, while over four hundred Tlingit had been baptized in Sitka prior to 1867, their knowledge of, and commitment to, Orthodoxy was quite weak, and it declined even further after the sale of Alaska. The historical reasons for this sudden change in the Tlingit attitude toward Orthodoxy, which caught the Russian missionaries by surprise, are examined in detail in two of my recent papers (Kan 1983, 1984), but a brief discussion of this subject is needed here.

In the late 1870s and the early 1880s, while Orthodox missionary work among the Tlingit came almost to a standstill, a newly established Presbyterian mission experienced considerable success. In Sitka it opened a boarding school for the native children and established a Presbyterian church, with the majority of its members recruited from among the Tlingit. Some of them were attracted by the novelty of the church, others hoped to benefit from it materially, while many probably hoped that they could acquire some of the newcomers' power by learning to pray and sing. Many of the first members of that church were students of the Sitka Industrial School (run by the Presbyterian mission) and their relatives from the Sitka Indian village, called the "Ranche" by the white population. While many Tlingit parents were interested in having their children learn to read, write, and speak the language of the whites so as to compete with them successfully in the economic sphere, they resented the forced school attendance and other forms of Presbyterian pressure, including a prohibition on speaking Tlingit in the school and attacks on potlatches, shamanism, and other traditional native beliefs and ritual practices. In fact, the entire Tlingit way of life, from communal living in lineage houses to the use of bodily adornment, came under fire from the Presbyterians supported by military and civil authorities. Finally, Tlingit members of the Presbyterian Church soon realized that being Protestants did not automatically give them a respectable position in Sitka's society and protect them from discrimination. As a matter of fact, several Presbyterian leaders, and their supporters in the local government, including the future Governor of Alaska, John G. Brady, became involved in various abuses of the natives, including taking over their land, exploitation of their natural resources, and so forth.

In addition, Presbyterian ministers, such as A. Austin, made frequent attacks on the Orthodox Church and tried hard to convince the Orthodox Indians to abandon their faith and become Protestant (see Appendix #10). To counteract this campaign, the Russian Church began to appeal to the U.S. government in Washington as well as to the Russian ambassador on behalf of its native parishioners (see Appendices #10-12). Of course, in its defense of the Tlingit from economic exploitation, forced school attendance, Presbyterian propaganda, and other abuses, the Orthodox Church was protecting its own interests. Nevertheless, its special status in Alaska after 1867, ambivalence about the Americanization of the Creoles and the Indians, as well as a somewhat greater tolerance of native customs, encouraged Tlingit conversion to Orthodoxy during the time when Christianity had already become attractive to them but Presbyterianism seemed too oppressive to the majority. There were other reasons for this sudden movement toward Orthodoxy, such as its greater use of the native language in services and instruction, a much more elaborate ritual, involving the use of sacred objects and potent substances (holy water, icons, candles, etc.), as well as a certain compatibility between the Orthodox and the traditional Tlingit mortuary rituals and attitudes toward the dead. Orthodoxy appealed particularly to the more conservative, less acculturated Tlingit who resided in the Sitka village and several neighboring communities, such as Killisnoo, Angoon, Hoonah, and Juneau. Sitka parish statistics speak for themselves. While in 1882 there were 117 Tlingit members in the church, their number rose to 320 (or 330) in 1886, 700 in 1887, and between 800 and 900 in 1892.[7] Prior to Kamenskii's arrival in Sitka, Orthodoxy had already spread not only to the communities mentioned above but to such distant villages as Yakutat, Klukwaan, and even Atlin in the Yukon Territory.

While the number of converts was quite impressive, their knowledge and understanding of the Orthodox dogma and ritual were rather rudimentary, whereas their commitment to traditional ways of thinking and living remained quite strong. Fr. Anatolii saw his major task as a missionary to combat what he called "the two greatest evils of native life"—intemperance and the "clan-based mode of life." In addition, he was strongly committed to defending the Tlingit from Presbyterian abuses (see Appendix #10). To understand Kamenskii's efforts one has to examine his and other Russian missionaries' views of the Tlingit culture as well as their approach to missionization. While it is true that, compared to Protestant missionaries, they were more tolerant of native customs, a view that they were strong supporters of indigenous cultures expressed in several recent studies (e.g., Smith 1980), needs to be qualified. Although the most enlightened among them, such as Bishop Innokentii Veniaminov, did encourage considerable tolerance of customs that did not contradict Orthodoxy and adaptation of church practices to local ecological and cultural conditions, not all of the missionaries actually put those instructions into practice.

In Russia itself the Orthodox approach to missionary work among the native peoples of Siberia and Central Asia vacillated between considerable tolerance and a wide use of local languages, and attacks on native cultures combined with an emphasis on Russification. Thus, for example, one well-known Siberian missionary, Bishop Veniamin of Irkutsk, wrote in 1885, that the essence and the purpose of the activity of Russian missionaries in Siberia consisted "not only of the struggle against alien religions, but against alien nationalities, mores, customs and the entire lifestyle of the natives..., so as to make them Russian, not only in their faith but in their nationality as well" (quoted in Vdovin 1979:5-6). On the other hand, students of a special missionary department opened in the Kasan' Theological Academy were taught "not to destroy pagan beliefs, but rather to try to bring them closer to Christianity, to Christianize them" (ibid.:57).

Of course, in American-owned Alaska, Russification of the natives was out of the question, but attacks on their "pagan" beliefs and ceremonies were not. Thus, while some Russian missionaries demonstrated ambivalent attitudes toward such a major Tlingit ceremony as the potlatch, Kamenskii himself found much to condemn in the Tlingit culture of the 1890s. To get a better understanding of his position, one has to turn to his book, his articles in the Orthodox press (e.g., "The Frog Case," Appendix #9), and the statutes of the Indian Temperance and Mutual Aid Society that he prepared (Appendix #5).

It is not surprising that the young Russian missionary attacked shamanism, belief in witchcraft, or memorial feasts for the dead, since those "pagan" beliefs and rituals obviously contradicted Orthodoxy.[8] His criticism of the Tlingit culture, however, was aimed at its entire foundation—the matrilineal system of descent and the extended family residing in a lineage-owned house. Kamenskii objected to this because he saw such practices as blood feuds, polygamy, and inheritance that deprived the widow and her children of the deceased man's estate as being based on the matrilineal principle of social organization. Of course, his ethnocentrism prevented Kamenskii from understanding that these survivors received generous compensation by the matrikin of the deceased and were cared for by their own maternal relatives. He was even able to connect the Tlingit refusal to marry according to the Christian rite to their commitment to the matrilineal system, i.e., their fear that children of a "legalized" marriage could claim their father's property and receive support in their claims from the missionaries and the American authorities.

Was there anything in the traditional Tlingit culture that Fr. Anatolii considered worth admiring and preserving? Like most Russian missionaries, including Bishop Innokentii, he admired their industriousness, hunting, fishing and commercial skills, excellent craftsmanship, physical stamina, and oratorical skills. He even admired the position of women in the Tlingit family and their treatment of children, with the exception of cold baths and whipping administered to young men by their maternal uncles.

His major point of disagreement with the Presbyterians on the future of the Tlingit was the economy, the way the natives were supposed to make a living. Unlike the Protestant missionaries, Kamenskii did not think that the Tlingit necessarily had to become carpenters, merchants, or farmers, i.e., to acquire "respectable" Western skills and trades. Instead, he believed that the traditional subsistence—hunting and fishing—was essential for the native socioeconomic survival and wellbeing. His program for the future of the native of southeastern Alaska (see Appendix #9) was a peculiar blend of ideas, with a clear influence of the Russian idealization of the patriarchal lifestyle of peasants, hunters, and fishermen, which was reflected in some of the major laws developed in the nineteenth century for the natives [*inorodtsy*] of Siberia by the Russian government.

While objecting to the establishment of large Indian reservations, like those that existed in the rest of the country, Kamenskii proposed to create native territorial enclaves closed to white hunters/fishermen and especially commercial companies, and ruled by individual communities (or communes, Russian *obshchestva*), under the leadership of the traditional elders and chiefs [*taiony*]. There is a certain inconsistency in this view, since Kamenskii himself frequently stated that the traditional aristocracy was the main defender of the "pagan customs." To weaken their influence over the rest of the Indians he proposed to give school teachers considerable power to interfere in local affairs. While in his book *Tlingit Indians of Alaska*, Fr. Anatolii suggested that the Tlingit would inevitably die out with the rest of the "Red Race," in his program for their future presented in the "Frog Case," he asserted his conviction that they would eventually become equal citizens of Alaska. In fact, he suggested that an Indian wishing to leave his commune and lead the life of a white man, should be allowed to do so and be given rights equal to the rest of the American population. Thus his model of Tlingit acculturation proposed a much more gradual transition from "savagery" to "civilization" than those suggested by his Presbyterian rivals.

In his practical efforts to encourage the "spiritual progress" of the native parishioners, Kamenskii used several methods. He conducted frequent lectures and talks [*besedy*] with the Tlingit, usually with the help of an interpreter. Like most Russian missionaries, he never learned to speak or even understand Tlingit, although his ethnographic works include a number of native terms.[9]

Fr. Anatolii also used his medical knowledge and a supply of medications purchased by the church to help the natives and attract new Tlingit members to Orthodoxy, and/or to keep them from defecting to the Presbyterian side, which had a full-time physician-surgeon, a nurse, and a hospital for its native members. Competition over patients and potential converts between the two missions was quite intense, which is mentioned in both the Orthodox missionary reports and the memoirs of a Presbyterian physician, Dr. Wilbur (n.d.:321-322): "Fr. Anatolius was a huge man, big and brawny, and in his robes and a high headdress looked tremendous. He was an untiring worker, in the Ranche constantly, and, while he told me he would not interfere with my patients, I found that he prescribed for anyone asking it." According to Fr. Anatolii's own testimony, Wilbur offered his service to the Orthodox Tlingit, but on the condition that they would convert to Presbyterianism. Both missionaries combined medical assistance with prayers, hoping to win new converts.

The two churches competed in the domain of Indian education as well. The Russian mission did not have the funds or the manpower to maintain a school comparable to the Industrial Training School organized by the Presbyterians in Sitka to teach large numbers of Tlingit students to become English-speaking, Protestant Americans, skilled in carpentry, printing, commerce, and other trades. These students were indoctrinated to be negative about their parents' way of life and encouraged to set up their own nuclear households in a cottage community built on the mission-owned land away from the "evil influence" of the "Ranche." In addition to the Industrial School, Presbyterian propaganda affected Tlingit students attending the public school as well, since many of its teachers were members of that church.

This explains why Kamenskii attacked Sheldon Jackson's system of the Protestant monopoly in Alaskan native education (Appendix #9; see also Hinckley 1982:236-262). To counteract this powerful influence he established a day school for the Tlingit children in Sitka in 1897 in a newly constructed building, at the entrance to the Tlingit village (Appendix #14). He also encouraged Indian education in other southeastern Alaskan parishes, and, according to Jackson's own Annual Reports on the Alaskan Education, Orthodox schools enjoyed considerable success among the Tlingit. Contrary to Presbyterian allegations, these schools taught not only Russian and Tlingit, but English as well. Despite a constant shortage of money, supplies, and staff, they managed to provide Tlingit youngsters with a basic secular and religious education.

Father Anatolii's other major accomplishment was the creation in 1896 of an Indian Society of Temperance and Mutual Aid (Appendices #5-8, 13-16). It was aimed at eradicating drinking and other new vices introduced by the white man, as well as fighting "pagan customs," while also promoting peace, mutual aid, Christian education and morality. At first it was not too popular, except with the younger, better-educated, and more acculturated Tlingit. Eventually, however, traditional aristocracy joined it and took over its leadership, bringing many new members, so that by 1902 there were 110 Tlingit in the Society, with that number rising to about 200 in the next decade.[10] Soon thereafter, Indian brotherhoods spread to other Tlingit communities and continued to be quite active until the 1940s-1950s. Gradually they became semi-independent native religious organizations that were the core of the Orthodox Tlingit parishes. Participation in these sodalities enabled the Tlingit to strengthen their position within the Russian Church and thereby establish a more balanced relationship with the Russian clergy and parishioners. It also prepared them for assuming control over the parish, when the Russian-Creole population began to die off, leave the Church, and become more Americanized (Kan 1984).

The major activities of these organizations included holiday banquets, processions to and from the church, with members dressed in special regalia, and very popular weekly "gospel" or "testimonial" meetings conducted in one of the brotherhood meeting houses in the villages. Frequently led by Tlingit religious leaders, rather than Russian clergymen, they were a blend of Orthodox and Protestant elements, much to the surprise of the Orthodox missionaries. Orthodox prayers were learned, the Bible read in Russian and translated into Tlingit, and elaborate "testimonial" confessions made by each participant. Traditionally fond of singing and public oratory, the Tlingit attended such gatherings quite well. It was in this context that most of them learned the basics of Orthodoxy and strengthened their commitment to the Russian Church. In addition, these organizations strengthened community ties and encouraged mutual aid and peace during the period when the traditional social organization began to decline and the nuclear family was slowly replacing it as the key social unit of daily life.[11] At the same time, Orthodox brotherhoods helped maintain the prestige and influence of the traditional aristocratic leadership, which was beginning to be challenged by the Americans and some of the more acculturated, prosperous, younger men of the lower rank, who enriched themselves working in the mines and the canneries. Finally, brotherhoods improved the image of the Tlingit in the eyes of the local American population and helped reduce intemperance to a certain extent.

While the missionary reports translated here emphasize the achievements of the Indian brotherhoods in combating "paganism," other ethnographic and historical evidence indicates that the majority of the Orthodox Tlingit remained strongly committed to some of the fundamental beliefs, values, and rituals of their traditional culture, including the potlatch, one of the main subjects of missionary attacks. In several Tlingit communities today, especially in Sitka, the elderly Orthodox people still constitute the core of the more traditionalist population, while many of the Presbyterian natives have been forced to give up a lot more of their heritage.

In recent publications (1983, 1984), I have argued that Orthodoxy was more popular among the more conservative, less acculturated Tlingit not so much because of its tolerance of indigenous customs and beliefs, but because Russian missionaries lacked the power to fight them, did not want to appear as demanding as their Presbyterian rivals, and were less committed to Westernizing the Indians. Particularly important was the fact that Orthodoxy offered a much more elaborate ceremonial system to a people that valued ritual, sacred artifacts, singing, etc. Unlike the Protestant service involving the sermon and the reading of the Bible and, hence, inaccessible to many older, non-schooled Tlingit, the Orthodox liturgy was meaningful to the natives of different backgrounds, although the meaning they attributed to Orthodox communion, baptism, icons, and so on, was often quite different from what the Russian missionaries preached.

The Orthodox Church provided symbolic forms of which the Tlingit were able to take advantage to justify and preserve some of the essential aspects of their traditional culture, in a modified form, of course (Kan 1983, 1984). Consequently, culture change took place at a much slower pace and was less painful, sometimes without even being perceived as change. Thus, I would argue, instead of seeing Russian missionaries as solely responsible for this, we should instead appreciate the Tlingit ingenuity in being able to "indigenize" Christianity, to reinterpret it to fit their own patterns of thought. While missionaries contributed to this process by using the native language as a means of religious instruction and translating some of the major prayers into it, much of this syncretism took place in spite of their efforts and without their full comprehension.

Let us now return to Fr. Anatolii Kamenskii's biography and also examine his major contributions to Tlingit ethnography. His labors in Alaska were not easy. In fact, confrontations occurred not only with the Presbyterians and government officials (see Appendix #10), but with members of his own parishes—an influential Sitka merchant and the church warden [*starosta*], Sergei Kostromitinov, the Russians and Creoles resentful of his concern with the Tlingit, clergymen engaged in drinking and disobeying his authority, and, finally, the Indians themselves who refused to marry in the Church, persisted in potlatching, and so forth. In a number of letters addressed to the Bishop of Alaska, Nikolai (Ziorov), Kamenskii complained about his bad health, being overworked, not getting along with some of the leading parishioners, and a general depressed state of mind. One year after his arrival in Sitka, he was already asking to be transferred to other parishes, including San Francisco, Galveston, Texas, and especially Russia. He mentions missing his motherland and says that serving in an isolated Siberian parish would be preferable to remaining in Alaska. In one letter, he speaks about his fear of dying in a foreign land. Financial difficulty was another constant problem. His modest salary was barely enough to support one person, but Kamenskii was also sending money to his brother, a seminary student in Russia.

Despite such complaints, the Church rewarded Kamenskii for outstanding missionary work by making him an archimandrite in 1897. The same year he was promised to be relieved of his duties in Alaska, as soon as his replacement would arrive. This did not happen until 1898, when, instead of sending him home, the Church ordered Kamenskii to travel to Minneapolis to become the principal of a recently established parish school and an orphange. He remained in Minnesota for five years, actively engaged in strengthening Orthodox education. Shortage of funds forced him to teach most of the subjects in the school, while also acting as its administrator and treasurer. According to his colleague, Professor Paul Zaichenko (Tarasar 1975:80), Fr. Anatolii was very popular among his students and lent books freely to them from his personal library. In addition, he continued writing for the American Orthodox press and participated in the Russian-American Mutual Aid Society. His school became known as one of the best Orthodox educational institutions in North America. While Minneapolis was probably a more comfortable place to live than Sitka, Kamenskii was still overburdened with work and was finally allowed to return to Russia in February of 1903. He boarded a ship in New York on February 23 with a bouquet of flowers presented to him by members of the local Orthodox parish (*Russian Orthodox American Messenger*, 1903, vol. 7, no. 6:90-92).

We know little about his subsequent career in Russia, except that he became the rector of the Odessa Seminary, and in 1904-1907 delivered three lectures to the students of one of the Odessa high schools on the subject of Orthodoxy in America. They were published in Odessa in 1908 under the title "Sketches of an Archipastor." There is no information on whether Kamenskii survived the tragic years of the 1917 Revolution, the Civil War, and the Soviet campaign of extermination of Orthodox clergymen.

We also do not know when he began recording his observations of Tlingit customs. His first work on that subject was published in New York in 1899 by the *Russian Orthodox American Messenger* and was entitled *The Indian Tribe of Tlingit*. It contained the first four chapters of his later monograph on Tlingit culture that appeared in Russia in 1906. In 1900-1902 Kamenskii published a series of articles in the *Russian Orthodox American Messenger* under a general title "The Ancient Religion of the Tlingit," which formed the core of the remaining portion of the 1906 book *Tlingit Indians of Alaska*.

How can we evaluate Fr. Anatolii Kamenskii's ethnographic work? To begin with, it is essential to understand his theoretical position and biases, which influenced the selection and presentation of ethnographic data. Kamenskii was quite explicit about his views on the development of primitive religion and society. As a Christian missionary, he was particularly concerned with native religion, since understanding it was essential for fighting against it. Like his predecessor Bishop Innokentii Veniaminov, he provided detailed information on Tlingit shamanism, witchcraft, beliefs about spirits, mythology, and other aspects of the indigenous religion. His data supplement the earlier accounts of Russian travellers (Lisianskii, Litke), Russian-American Company officials (Khlebnikov), and missionaries (Veniaminov), as well as European naturalists (Krause) and American anthropologists (Swanton, Oberg, Olson, de Laguna).

Some of the ethnographic data he collected are of special value, e.g., description of the ceremony accompanying a volcanic eruption or an earthquake, account of the mortuary ritual, new versions of various myths, including those about the Raven, the Old Woman Underneath the Earth, and the Tl'anaxéedákw. In fact, Kamenskii's description of Tlingit religion is much more detailed than that of Krause (1885) and is comparable to that of Swanton (1908). At the same time he barely mentions the central Tlingit ceremony—the potlatch. Most likely, being a missionary, he could not attend one, while his native informants were probably reluctant to discuss the potlatch with a man who condemned it in his sermons.

The weakest aspect of Kamenskii's discussion of Tlingit religion is his attempt to find traces of monotheism in it, by going as far as using a missionary-introduced term Dikée Aanakáawu to support his argument. Equally fallacious is his claim that Yéil, Xeitl and other mythological protagonists had once been worshipped as gods. The entire scheme underlying his presentation of data on indigenous religion is explicitly stated in Chapter 5 of the *Tlingit Indians of Alaska.* One could call it a theory of degeneration of Tlingit religion, a decline from primitive monotheism, to polytheism, to nature worship, to beliefs about spirits of the dead and of animals, and finally to shamanism and witchcraft. While the author's references to various world religions indicated his erudition, they failed to support the general argument. Such a dogmatic approach led to occasional distortion of data, mistakes, and misinterpretations.

Kamenskii's position on the subject of primitive religion should not surprise us, since he was a Christian scholar. After all, such a well-known Christian ethnologist as Wilhelm Schmidt and a major Russian theologian and philosopher Vladimir Solov'ev (whose influence on Kamenskii is clear) subscribed to a similar theory. More interesting and unusual is the fact that Kamenskii combined this Christian view of primitive religion with an evolutionary theory of the development of society. His understanding of the Tlingit family, clan, and other aspects of the indigenous social organization, was influenced by Morgan as well as other evolutionary ethnologists, such as Tylor and Lippert. He obviously read their works in America or in Russia, borrowed some of their terminology, and saw his own account as contributing to the general picture of the evolutionary development of mankind from "savagery," to "barbarism," to "civilization" (see Morgan 1877). Kamenskii's high opinion of Morgan was probably due not only to his view that the New York lawyer was the leading ethnological authority on American Indians, but to Morgan's great popularity in Russia in the last decades of the nineteenth century.

Fortunately, Kamenskii's evolutionism did not interfere too much with his presentation of ethnographic data on Tlingit social life. The information he provided is an important bridge between the earlier Russian accounts and the turn of the century American ethnographic works on Tlingit society. Kamenskii's discussion of the process of selection of lineage and clan leaders, and the Tlingit system of payment by means of blankets is a unique account of social phenomena overlooked by other observers of the period.

One of the major strengths of the *Tlingit Indians of Alaska* was its historical dimension. Unlike such Boasians as Swanton and Olson, Kamenskii described the Tlingit culture of a particular period—the end of the nineteenth century—rather than presenting an historical account of a "memory culture." Throughout his study, one finds frequent references to changes brought about by European and especially American influence. Thus, for example, he reported the role played by European regalia and written certificates, treated by the Tlingit as valuable prestige objects and transmitted along with traditional ceremonial objects through the maternal line. He commented on the decline of the power of the traditional aristocracy, caused by the American reliance on Indian policemen, some of whom were recruited from the lower ranks of the native society. In addition, information on such important historical events as the dispute between two of Sitka's clans over a crest, or the fate of a Kaagwaantaan ceremonial staff is very important for the study of Tlingit culture change that occurred at the end of the nineteenth century.

While Kamenskii's ethnographic work had many strong aspects, it also contained a number of weaknesses. The author was at his best when he simply reported what he observed or learned from the Tlingit, but when he ventured into speculations and hypothesizing, he produced some rather far-fetched conclusions. Thus, it is difficult to accept his theory that it was intertribal war that brought the Tlingit to southeastern Alaska or that they had arrived in the area only a few centuries prior to the Europeans. While his view on the similarity between the Tlingit and Siberian shamanism has a certain validity, it is impossible to accept the assertion that the Iroquois and the Tlingit cultures were basically alike. Of course, such sweeping generalizations stemmed from the author's evolutionism, his idea about the cultural unity of the "Red Race," and a rather limited knowledge of the ethnographic literature on North American Indians. While Kamenskii mentions having read Morgan, Bancroft and Prescott, there is no evidence of his familiarity with the works of the Bureau of American Ethnology, which explains his surprising assertion that the literature on the subject was quite limited.

His outline of the history of the Russian colonization of southeastern Alaska also contained inaccuracies, and suggested that he had not read any major primary sources on the subject. While Fr. Anatolii's description of native subsistence and material culture is adequate, although not comparable to a detailed account by Krause (1885), his discussion of the Tlingit language leaves much to be desired, especially if compared to the works of Veniaminov (1840), Swanton (1908), and even Krause (ibid.).

In evaluating Kamenskii's work one should bear in mind that it was not intended to be a scholarly publication, but a more popular reading for both scholars and the general public, including missionaries. One finds no footnotes, references to other sources,[12] or a bibliography. The writing style is not scholarly either, but rather colloquial, with occasional flowery passages and some sensationalist remarks about the "savage" nature of the past Tlingit life (e.g., the description of the violent and bloody fights between Tlingit women).

Despite such shortcomings, Fr. Anatolii Kamenskii's ethnographic work represents an important source of information on Tlingit culture of the period and stands out among the best Russian missionary accounts of native cultures of Siberia and Alaska. For a person without any professional training in anthropology or linguistics, Kamenskii was able to produce a fairly detailed, accurate, and well-rounded description of a native Alaskan culture in a state of change caused by Western colonization.

For the present-day reader, it is an interesting document not only for its value as an early ethnography, but as an example of the views of an Orthodox missionary on the people among whom he was laboring. Combined with other writings by Kamenskii and his Orthodox co-workers, translated here, it provides essential data for a study of the relationship between theory and practice in the work of Russian missionaries at the turn of the century. It dispells an erroneous view of them being tolerant cultural relativists and, instead, portrays them as human beings of their own times, and with their own cultural and personal biases and illusions. At the same time, it reveals some significant differences between their views of and approaches to Alaskan natives and those of their Protestant American rivals (cf. Jones 1914), and thus helps one understand the history of Christian missionization of Alaska.

It is my hope that by introducing these new ethnographic and historical documents to the general public (including descendants of the people described by Fr. Anatolii Kamenskii), and scholars, valuable new information on subjects of considerable interest will be provided.

NOTES

1. The complete title of this book is *In the Land of Shamans. Indians of Alaska. Their Social Life and Religion.*

2. There have been several versions of the English translation of Bishop Innokentii's monograph, the most recent and authoritative one being that of Lydia Black, published by The Limestone Press (Richard A. Pierce, editor).

3. In my Ph.D. thesis (1982) on Tlingit mortuary and memorial ritual, Kamenskii's data have also been used.

4. The article was entitled "Fr. Archimandrite Anatolii's Departure for Russia" and appeared in vol. 7, no. 6, pp. 90-92 of this journal.

5. Published in Odessa in 1908, they were entitled "Sketches of an Archipastor" and included the following lectures: "Orthodoxy in America," "Slavic People in America" and "The Question of Religion in America."

6. Throughout this work, the Alaska Church Collection is referred to as "ACC," while the accompanying code indicates the file number.

7. The last figure includes residents of several neighboring villages who came to Sitka to be baptized.

8. It was only in the 1960s that the Alaska Orthodox Church officially adopted a much more tolerant attitude toward native customs (see Tarasar 1975: 291-293; Smith 1980:15-16).

9. Kamenskii frequently complained to his superior about the difficulties of working with the Tlingit without a reliable native interpreter.

10. In 1904 St. Michael Brotherhood was divided into two organizations, with an offshoot taking the name of St. Gabriel. The main cause of this split was a conflict between the two clans of the Raven moiety described in Kamenskii's monograph and other documents translated here.

11. Matrilineal groups have continued to play the key role in the native ceremonial life to the present.

12. Despite the lack of references, several passages in the book are clearly based on the work of Veniaminov and possibly other Russian sources, such as Khlebnikov's (1835) biography of Baranov.

TLINGIT INDIANS OF ALASKA
Odessa, 1906

Archimandrite Anatolii Kamenskii

INTRODUCTION : CURRICULUM
OF THE BOOK'S GENESIS

The origin of this book is the following. Several years ago its author happened to live in Alaska among the natives. Missionary work frequently brought him into contact with these semisavage*¹ [Tlingit] Indians and he compiled brief notes based on daily observations of their life. As a missionary, the author was primarily interested in Indian customs and beliefs, and generally in everything that was, in one way or another, connected with their religious ideas, ancient and present.

The only thing we, the Russians, usually know about the American aborigines is what we learn from short geographic manuals and fantastic novels by Mayne Reid,*² Cooper and others. Our knowledge does not extend beyond these works of fiction aimed mainly at young people. Whole generations have grown up and aged with these books and with the image of America as a kingdom of bloodthirsty redskins, headhunters, and so forth. Somehow these notions peacefully coexist in our imagination with equally fantastic stories about the cultural miracles of the New World—the odd and brilliant Yankees, twenty-story buildings, etc. It is as if the bloodthirsty Indians of the prairies and the smart Yankee were brothers. The last of the Mohicans and Sherlock Holmes*³—what is, after all, the difference between them?

With such superficial ideas, I landed in the New World. At first, however, I managed to see only the civilized Yankees and not the Indians. Only after crossing the whole continent, in the state of Wyoming, did I manage to see the redskins with their mustangs, moccasins, etc. This was a very brief encounter, until our train stopped at one of the stations in the so-called Central Indian Desert.*⁴ After that the kingdom of culture resumed, with our final destination in San Francisco. And only after sailing for seven more days, did I find myself among the insular Indians.*⁵ With great attention, I began observing the life of these redskins. Images of Cooper's and Mayne Reid's Indians kept rushing through my head. I compared those images with these real examples of the remnants of the red race. My book became the result of this comparison.

I must admit it was difficult to make sense of the material I was accumulating daily. After all, I was living on a semi-wild island in the Bering Sea [?] thousands of *verstas* away from civilization, from libraries, deprived of an opportunity to look for needed references in books on the social life and religion of savages and specifically Indians. This fact, of course, had a negative impact on the book. On the other hand, however, when the material organized in its present form was finally verified, it turned out that the information about the social life and religion of American Indians was rather limited. Some data on Mexican Indians, that have disappeared off the face of the earth a long time ago, could be found in Prescott; [Friedrich] Muller, Reville, Bancroft, and several other authors provide some additional information. The most fundamental work, however, is Morgan's book *Ancient Society* which pays special attention to Indian tribes of North America. The reader might benefit from getting acquainted with some of the opinions of Morgan's book.[1],[6]

Racial Unity and the Great Value of the Material

Even these brief facts hastily pulled out of Morgan's work are sufficient to prove the close affinity between the Indians of the continent and the islands. And if one adds to this some of the data gathered by Ebrard[7] in his Apologetik, i.e., the so-called "Legends of the Redskins" about the flood, the creation of the world, the fall of man, etc., and then takes into consideration the obvious similarity between them in physical appearance, clothing, governments, methods of skin-dressing for household use, basket weaving, carving of one's genealogies on wood and the system of totems in general, and finally, the similarity between their languages—there is no longer any doubt about the existence of tribal and cultural unity between the two Indian groups. Even the ancient extinct Mexican Indians and the Aztecs cannot be excluded from this unity.

And if it is an established fact, then the whole material brought together in our book acquires a great value, since these data can be used to judge many aspects of the life of the whole red race, so poorly studied and destined to disappear completely off the face of the earth, before science has the time to become acquainted with its history, social organization, customs, morals, and religious beliefs. At the same time, this book will offer at least a little bit of new information that will enrich the entire science of the history of primitive culture. After all, most of the so-called scholarly conclusions about the mythology, philosophy, and religion of primitive peoples have been made on the basis of the same type of fragmentary, scattered, and not always definitely verified facts collected at different times by different people. When one reads the works of E.B. Tylor, J. Lippert, and others, with their broad generalizations about the culture of the peoples in a state of savagery or barbarianism, or the book by R. de la Grasserie[8] delving into primitive psychology, on every page one finds proof of the importance of single facts for the scholar weaving his scientific cloth and, like a mosaic maker who carefully chooses certain shades and colors, selecting those facts that fit his conclusions.

In addition, certain peculiar characteristics of the religious beliefs and notions of the people of the red race are valuable because they make it easier to prove the absolute truth of the idea that the religious systems of mankind have one single source. Consequently certain stages of development of one or another branch of mankind are characterized by the same forms of religion, e.g., shamanism is equally present among the dying races of northern Russia and northern Siberia as well as Indian tribes. The law of atavism whose irrepressible force has led to the continuing degeneration of many peoples of the Old and the New World, manifests itself with a special strength in the sphere of religion. Due to this law, the red race has almost totally died out. But it has left a trace behind: the study of Indian religious beliefs and notions destroys the most recent theories of the origin of pagan religions—animism and naturism—developed by the students of the history of culture.[2,*9]

But *sat sapienti*. Every book has to speak for itself.

CHAPTER I

Settlements of the Tlingit Indians. The First Russian Encounter with Them One Hundred Years Ago. Warfare and Hunting. Language as an Indicator of the Development of Culture.

Among the various native tribes inhabiting Alaska, there is one calling itself "Tlingit," which means "people." By this the Tlingit imply that only those belonging to their tribe are true human beings, free and independent, similar to the Hebrews who in ancient times designated themselves *God's Chosen People.* The first Russian visitors to Alaska named them the *Kaliuzh* or the *Kolosh,*[10] and even now they are occasionally called so. But it would be more correct to call them the Alaskan or the Maritime Indians as they are usually labelled by the Americans, since they undoubtedly belong to the same ethnic group as the nomadic Indians of Canada and the United States.

The geographical location of the settlements of these Indians is the southeastern coast of the Alaskan mainland between longitude 128° and 145° W. and latitude 50° and 60° N., and mostly such large islands adjacent to it as Chichagof, Baranof, Admiralty, Kupreanof, and Prince of Wales. The major Indian settlements within this area are located in Sitka, Killisnoo, Hoonah, Khootznahoo, Chilkat, Yakutat, Wrangell, Kake, Taku, Juneau, etc. These settlements are the continuation of similar ones inhabited by other Indian tribes: Haida, Tsimshian, Tanana, and others extending to Canada and the U.S. The "Tlingit" were probably a vanguard tribe moving from east to west along the endless American plains. This movement might have been part of a wider migration of Indian tribes from the Atlantic to the Pacific shores, which began with the arrival of the white people to the New World. Most likely, however, it was stimulated by the general cause of any migration, i.e., internecine war. The defeated tribes, pushed to the sea, had to seek refuge on the islands. They found it here in the quiet coves and inlets, almost inaccessible to the enemy. All of these islands are covered with impassable forests, as well as mountain ranges where the snow never melts. The climate is severe, but there is plenty of game in the forests and fish are abundant in the lakes and bays. The latter conditions could also have had an influence on the Indian migration.

It is difficult to establish the exact time of the Tlingit arrival in Alaska, but in any case, it took place not too long ago (about four or five hundred years).[11] However, we have no evidence for tracing their way of life back to more than a century, i.e., prior to the time when the first Russian *promyshlenniki* came to Alaska. But even these data are relatively scarce. The first Russian encounter with the Tlingit dates back to the end of the 1790s.[12] The Russians found them already acquainted with the Europeans. The first Europeans who visited them for trading purposes were probably the Spanish. At least such a legend exists among the Indians. Later on, following the Spanish, the Indian waters were frequented by the British and the Americans from Boston, which explains why the Tlingit still refer to the latter as "Bostonians.""[13] This acquaintance with the whites, however, began only some ten or fifteen years prior to the Russian arrival.

The first time the Russians came face to face with the "Kaliuzh" was in June of 1792, when Baranov was staying with a hunting party in Nuchek Bay [Port Etches]. The Kaliuzh themselves arrived there together with the *Ugalentsy* [Eyak] from Yakutat Bay to take their revenge on the Chugach [Eskimos] for an offense of the previous year. Having suddenly stumbled on the Russian camp, they decided to challenge them. During the night they attacked Baranov's camp but were defeated. In 1796, Captain Shil'ts [Shields] cruised Chilkat Bay [Lynn Canal] and Sitka Bay [Sitka Sound], and in 1799-1800, Baranov himself built the first Russian fortified settlement among the Tlingit Indians.[14]

Although at that time Indian settlements were more populous, the Indians were more inclined toward a nomadic way of life.[15] They dwelled in large earth-covered *baraboras*, which one entered through a small semicircular opening, instead of a door, covered with a piece of hide during cold weather. A fire was lit in the middle of such a *barabora*, with the smoke escaping through this opening. Animal skins were used for clothing as well as bedding. Theirs was an austere way of life. The greater part of the year was spent in military expeditions against the neighboring Aleuts[16] and in internecine feuds. Warfare was considered the most honorable activity. Being fearless, they, like the ancient Vikings, often undertook seafaring expeditions in their *iaks* [*yaakw*] (huge canoes hollowed out of a single tree trunk), covering great distances. Under favorable weather conditions they covered between 150 to 200 miles, or about 300 *verstas* in twenty-four hours. Their war canoes could accommodate more than 40 well-armed warriors.

Prior to acquaintance with European firearms, their major weaponry consisted, as among other savages, of the bow and arrow.[17] Arrowheads were made of stone and bone; later on—after the Tlingit had become familiar with copper[18] and other metals—they began making metal ones. According to their legend, they saw copper for the first time when a Spanish vessel was wrecked near their shores. The nails from the ship were used by the Indians to make the first metal objects. Later on, iron was used for the same purpose. Besides the bow and arrow, every Tlingit carried a big dagger, originally made of bone or stone and later on of metal. This dagger was always worn around the neck. The armor included a tight suit made of thick leather and a short cuirass skillfully woven out of tree roots [wooden rods or staves]. A small round shield was made of the same material and fish [whale] sinews. Several cuirasses were sometimes worn one on top of the other. Over the cuirass a thick cloak was sometimes worn as

28

well. Instead of a helmet and visor a warrior wore a wooden headdress with a mask that had holes for the eyes and the mouth only. This mask would represent a certain animal, bird, or fantastic monster. Here is how Baranov describes the Tlingit armor and their military tactics, in one of the letters dealing with his first encounter with them in Nuchek Bay [Port Etches] in 1972.[19] "In the dark of the night, before dawn, we were surrounded by a multitude of armed warriors and a slaughter of natives (Aleuts present in Baranov's camp) began everywhere . . . Two of our men, who suddenly awoke, were killed. Although fewer people were on guard, darkness allowed the Indians to crawl up so close that we noticed them when they were already within ten paces, striking at our tents with their weapons. We were firing our rifles for a long time but without success, since they were wearing three or four layers of *kuiaks* [suits of armor made of wooden staves and plaited with sinew] and on top of that were covered with very thick moose cloaks. On their heads they wore thick *shishaks* [helmets] depicting various monsters, which none of our bullets or grape shot could penetrate. And indeed in that darkness they seemed to us more terrifying than the most awful devils of hell. They were approaching us, keeping a perfect order and obeying only the voice of their leader, while some of them were running back and forth, causing us and our natives harm. Thus they spent two hours, while we kept firing at them until dawn, when they finally stopped and began to retreat, but were still threatening to attack us again . . . ."

Sitka Museum [Sheldon Jackson Museum] contains a good number of ancient Indian weapons. Frequently, an Indian warrior was also armed with a short spear that had a wide sharp point. In the old days, a tambourine or a drum of special construction was indispensable in any military expedition.[20] Today they are used by Indians in war dances. The Alaskan Indians were not strangers to the custom of scalping their dead enemies during war raids. Many Indians still keep these trophies of the glorious adventures of their wild and ferocious ancestors. The most highly treasured are the scalps of white women.

Love of warfare was highly developed among the Tlingit. Endless wars were waged not only against various neighboring Aleut and Eskimo tribes but among themselves as well. The main cause of such bellicosity was the fact that the law of the blood feud—"an eye for an eye, a tooth for a tooth"—reigned supreme and was strictly observed. An offense was always punished by another offense, a wound by a wound, a death by a death. Nephews avenged for an injury of their maternal uncle, while their own injuries were in turn avenged by their maternal nephews. And thus vengeance continued from generation to generation within the clan, as long as at least one of its members remained alive. Not a single insult or injury was ever forgiven or forgotten.

Sometimes warfare provided the Tlingit with considerable booty, mainly in the form of slaves. Slavery was highly developed among them. The Tlingit himself considered it demeaning to perform dirty work around his *barabora*: this was the duty of slaves or at least of women.[21] When not engaged in warfare, most of their time was spent hunting land and sea animals. This activity demanded the same abilities as warfare: endurance, personal courage, cunning, and skills in catching animals and, at the same time, overcoming all the difficulties and obstacles caused by the local terrain and severe climate. Until the Tlingit became acquainted with the Europeans and learned the value of furs of such animals as beaver, otter, fur seal, marten, etc., they hunted only those animals which provided them with food, clothing, and other materials useful in the household. Because of that, among the land animals, they hunted moose (*tsisk*) [*dzisk'w*], bear, local deer (*kavokan*) [*guwakaan*] and certain types of mountain goat, and, among sea animals, seal [*nerpa*] and whale, since they provided enormous amounts of grease—a necessary nutrition in cold climate. Cereals were unknown. This type of food was substituted, to some extent, by various berries, including *shiksha* [crowberry, *Empetrum nigrum*], *moroshka* [salmonberry, *Rubus spectabilis* or cloudberry, *Rubus chamaemorus*], etc. All foods are prepared in grease. Even today the greatest delicacies are fermented fish and deer heads. These dishes are prepared in the following way: fresh fish and deer heads are wrapped in large *lopushnik* [burdock] leaves and buried in the ground exposed to the sun. They remain there for three or four days, until the smell of decomposition is detected, and then this delicacy is dug out and carefully licked all around. The brains turned green are considered the tastiest portion. Of course one has to get accustomed even to being present at such a meal. Their daily ration, however, consists of dried fish, or *iukola*, with its own peculiar smell, which serves the same purpose as bread among the Europeans. It is usually eaten dipped in fish oil or seal grease.

Because two kinds of animals were hunted, an Indian, beginning in early childhood, learned to climb mountain cliffs and canyons covered with virgin forest, with barely visible paths made by animals. From the early years, he had to learn to endure cold, dampness, and various changes of weather. For this purpose, on cold winter days, fathers brought their small children to the shore and threw them far into the sea.[22] This was performed during the coldest mornings. When the child came out of the water, the father whipped his body with spruce branches before allowing him to run to the fire after such a terrible bath. Young men, however, willingly organize such baths without waiting for orders from the elders. Apparently, Indian upbringing was even more severe than among the ancient Spartans.

At sea even greater difficulties and surprises awaited the Indian hunter. The Alaskan sea is stormy and menacing almost all year round. Often there are violent storms with terrifying winds. Huge foaming waves rush to the shore and crash with thundering noise against the rocks. This can terrify any mortal. One should pity the unfortunate person who dares resist its power and fight it. Meanwhile the Indian hunter frequently has to fight these elements. He has learned to survive both on land and at sea. On land the Indian fearlessly meets the black bear face to face, armed only with a dagger [spear?] and aided by small but agile and vicious small dogs. For travelling over water he has a special canoe which allows him to go into the open sea. When necessary, he can go without food for several days in a row. He is brave and resourceful in difficult circumstances. The Indian is not afraid of death and faces it in cold blood, although there are other reasons for this, as we shall see below.

It is likely that due to these and other conditions of his past life, the Tlingit Indian has developed certain characteristics, somewhat different from all the other types of northern natives as well as those of the American mainland. The Alaskan Indian or the Tlingit is tall, often over six feet; he has a long, almost round trunk, well-developed chest and arms, and legs slightly bent outward, as is typical among the true riders of the steppes. However, this curvature of the legs could have been caused by constant sitting inside a narrow boat. His gait is slow and ungainly, with some bending from side to side. The male gait is tolerable, but the female one is utterly ugly, especially when women try to walk fast. It resembles that of ducks or penguins. While men spend the greater part of the year outside the house in warfare and hunting, women remain permanently at home occupied with housework. Using spruce roots they weave *shkats*[23] or baskets of various shapes (which serve as their dishes and for transporting goods), dress and sew skins, etc. The assiduousness and patience of the women are amazing. All these activities are performed while sitting on the floor with legs tucked under. Such a sitting posture among pregnant women is especially harmful since it affects the fetus. Only the sedentary life of the Indian women can explain the presence of a large number of Indians lame from birth because one of their legs is shorter than the other.[24]

The head, however, sits proudly on a thick neck above the wide and powerful shoulders, thus compensating for the ugliness of the lower part of the body. A typical Tlingit face is expressive, lively and has well-defined features. Most of the faces are round and beardless, but elongated, strong ones, with aquiline noses are not uncommon. The forehead is not high but quite wide, usually with a slightly rounded top. The eyes are slanted but not as much as among the Chinese or the Japanese. Not uncommon are regular [non-slanted] eyes. The facial muscles are mobile, especially during a lively conversation. Some of the faces are very handsome, particularly among women. In general, the physiognomy of these Indians does not reflect dullness and complete apathy as the faces of the northern savages often do.[25] Were it not for their skin color, which has a slight coppery tone, some of the stately Tlingit men or women could almost be taken for Europeans.

At the present time one finds among these Indians faces with Caucasian features, which is a result of close contacts with the Russians and Americans. But it would be unfair to consider them Indian, since this type does not show

31

any traces of savagery.

The Tlingit language—*Tlingit kenakh* [*Lingít x'éináx*]*[26]—requires special attention because of its uniqueness. When a Tlingit starts speaking and his speech
pours out in a continuous flow, you would be amazed by its music and your
unaccustomed ear would have difficulty listening. And the Tlingit certainly love
to speak. Their speech is flowery and rich in imagery, and they are generally
good orators. Gestures and poses accompany their speeches. The language itself
is rich with words but even richer in grammatical forms. Nouns and adjectives
have articles, as in Greek; persons, tenses and moods of nouns and adjectives
are modified by means of prefixes. Europeans have great difficulty learning this
language. Its most difficult aspect is pronunciation. Many sounds cannot be
written or even pronounced. Listening carefully to the speech of a Tlingit, you
might hear the croaking of a frog, the bubbling of water, the cackling of a hen,
the crackle of breaking dry wood, or some guttural and rather pleasant, melodi-
ous sounds. One non-Orthodox missionary, describing his impressions of
Alaska, complained that here everybody and everything is afflicted by the
catarrh. Later on, discussing the Tlingit and their language, he adds that the
latter is the product of the local catarrhs—in other words, a "catarrhal" language.*[27] The characterization may contain some truth, but despite all that, it is
very pleasant to listen to a good Tlingit orator. In fact, the diversity of sounds
gives him an opportunity for a stronger and fuller expression of feelings and
thoughts.*[28]

Such advanced development of a language obviously testifies to the fact that
the people using it has existed for many centuries. On the other hand, this
presupposes the existence of more or less sophisticated forms of social and family
life, a variety of religious notions and other more or less complex aspects of
spiritual life. And, in fact, as we shall see below, the Tlingit do possess all of
these characteristics, which are as unique as their language.

CHAPTER II

Social Life. Tribes, Clans, Baraboras [Houses] or Families. Clan Symbols. Heads of Clans and Baraboras.

The social life and the social system of the Tlingit Indians resemble, to a degree, one of the forms of the traditional, semisavage state, which characterizes human life on the eve of the civilized era. Specifically, the Tlingit social life strongly resembles the biblical customs of the patriarchs of the Old Testament. If the Indians of the American mainland are considered by some scholars and by Mormons to be a branch of the Israelite people who had long ago migrated to the New World, one could make an even stronger argument in favor of the Tlingit Indians.

The kinship system is the foundation of the Tlingit social life. All the Tlingit are divided into two tribes,[29] each tribe in turn is divided into several clans, and each clan into *baraboras*[30] or families. The Raven tribe (or *Yeil*, in the Tlingit language) is considered to be older and more numerous.[31] The *Kiksady* [Kiks.ádi] or *Khikhchaty* (i.e., the frog clan) claim to be the oldest and the most powerful clan of this tribe.[32] Other clans of the Raven tribe are named after [or use the emblems of] the *kiziuch* [coho salmon], *sivuch* [sea lion], owl, etc.[33] According to widespread legends, the Wolf tribe considers the wolf or *kuch* [gooch] to be its ancestor. The clans of this tribe are named after [or use the emblems of] the bear, the eagle, the killer whale, the shark, etc. The most numerous clan of the Wolf tribe is *Kakvantan* [Kaagwaantaan] or *Kukhantan* [Kóok Hít Taan].[34]

There are very many clans in the two tribes and it is difficult to enumerate them all. The more outstanding ones among them are: *Tliukhanakhaty* [L'uknax.ádi], *Nushkitany* [Wooshkeetaan], *Kuchitany* [Goochhít Taan?], *Chakuneti* [Chookaneidí], *Tekvaty* [?], *Tekuiaty* [Teikweidí], *Atlentaany* [Aatleintaan ?], *Anikigaitany* [Aan.eegayaakhít Taan ?], *Khutsitany* [Xóots Hít Taan], *Nanaagi* [Naanyaa.aayí]. Almost all of these names were formed by adding the words *it* or *git* [hít]—"house," *barabora*, *an* [aan]—"village," *tan* [taan]—"owner" or "people of" to the names of animals, e.g., wolf—*kuch* [gooch], bear—*khuts* [xóots], coho salmon—*tliukh* [l'ook], eagle—*chak* [ch'áak'], shark [?].

Such an origin of the names allows one to think that all the clans were designated after one or another leader or head of the *barabora* who in turn was named after an animal. The origin of the names of the two tribes (Raven and Wolf) is probably the same. In time immemorial, there probably lived two men, one of whom was called *Yeil* and the other *Gooch*. Their descendants acquired the names of the Raven and the Wolf. At the same time, however, as they

33

multiplied, each descendant became the head of his own family, passing on his name to his descendants. This is how the aforesaid clans were formed. Members of a single clan usually dwell together in one village. Kiks.ádi, for example consider their ancestral home to be primarily the island of Sitka [Baranof Island]. Many of the L'uknax.ádi (a clan of the same tribe) also live in Sitka, but claim Yakutat Bay as their original home. The Kaagwaantaan are also considered to be newcomers in Sitka; their ancestral homes are in the village of old Hoonah and in Chilkat.

In every village, at the head of each clan there is a chief or *taion*, *ankau* [*aankáawu*], as they call him. The head of an important clan is called *atlen-ankau* [*aatlein aankáawu*]— the great [lit. "big"] chief. The other chiefs of the clan obey him. The title of a *taion* is both hereditary and elective. To become the head of a clan one has to belong to an ancient family or *barabora*, which counts many heroes among its ancestors. Usually the title of a chief is acquired in the following manner. Before the head of a *barabora* dies, he selects a successor to whom his title, all the attributes of his high position and most of his property are passed. The successor is selected not from the children or the brothers of the dying person but from his nephews—children of his sister. The title of the *taion* is passed on to his brothers, only when the testator has no sisters' sons or mother's sisters' daughters' sons. Furthermore, among the [maternal] nephews, it is the youngest who inherits and not the oldest.[35] This law, however, is not followed in all the clans and the *baraboras*. Sometimes the inheritance goes to the oldest [maternal] nephew.

This is the order of passing on the chieftaincy or leadership within the *barabora*. However, to become the *taion* of the clan one needs the consent of all its other *taions*, even if the dying is the leading *taion* who elevates his own successor to this position. Not infrequently there are claimants to clan chieftainship who belong to other *baraboras* and prevail over the heir, especially if he is young, inexperienced, and does not have a strong personality, while his rival, on the contrary, is a man widely known and respected among the members of his clan.

To elect a clan *taion* all the elders of the village [clan?] gather for a council.[36] Important councils among the Indians always take place in the dead of night. In these instances, noise and publicity are avoided. Neither women nor teenagers are allowed to attend. Prior to the council, the head of the *barabora* usually distributes tobacco and a period of silent smoking begins, resembling the "peace pipe" ceremony of mainland Indians. Then the person who is to be elected by the whole clan receives the regalia of the chiefly authority. Such regalia usually consisted of a long staff—*ankautsaka* [*aankáawu wootsaagáyi*], a ceremonial hat— *ankautsakhu* [*aankáawu s'áaxu*], various weapons, and the [ceremonial] garment of his heroic ancestors. The hat usually depicts the animal after which the clan is named.[37] The newly elected taion celebrates his ascendance to the new position by joyful dancing, during which he appears dressed in all the regalia of his rank and distributes gifts among the *taions* and high-ranking elders of other clans.*³⁸

Of all the chiefly regalia, the staff or the *ankautsaka* [*aankáawu wootsaagáyi*] is particularly important. It has a certain sacred quality and for that reason is used only on special occasions, such as during military councils when the *taion* takes his seat of honor among the people; in warfare when he commands the warriors of his clan; when he settles arguments and disputes between members of his clan; and often during big feasts. With this staff in his hand, the *taion* or the person whom he entrusts with it, can safely walk between the two lines of fighting warriors at the height of the battle and be sure that nobody would touch him because of his immunity. With this staff an envoy goes to the enemy camp to start peace negotiations.

The amount of respect paid to the *taion's* staff and its significance are directly proportional to its age. The older the staff, the more it is respected. One such staff is located in the Archaeological Museum of the St. Petersburg Theological Academy [*Dukhovnaia Akademiia*]. The staff is now over one hundred and twenty years old. It is made of poplar wood and has been painted dark brown (in more recent times). It is four and a half feet long and one and one-third inches wide. The top is decorated with twelve animal teeth fitted into the wood; about half a foot above the lower end, there is a carved figure of an anthropomorphic idol with pearl teeth and eyes. This staff was presented to the author by an Indian named Nikifor Kul'kita [Koolkéet'aa]. He became a member of the Orthodox Indian Temperance and Mutual Aid Society, founded in 1896, which has among its various goals the struggle against heathenism.*³⁹ Thus the staff was no longer of any use to him, especially since he had no direct heirs in his own family, which meant that when he died, it would have been transferred to another *barabora* or to the head *taion* of the whole clan. Here is, by the way, what he told me about this staff.

The first owner of the staff was Kunanek from the Kaagwaantaan clan. At that time the Kaagwaantaan were still living in their original home, in the old Hoonah village located on the other side of the straits across from the present site of Hoonah. This staff as well as the ceremonial hat (which is now in the possession of the head *taion* Khliantych [L.aanteech] was made to order by a L'uknax̱.ádi man named Stakvon [Sdaagwáan]. Before taking the staff in his hand and putting the hat on his head, Kunanek gave a big feast and invited guests from all the neighboring villages, such as Chilkat, Yakutat, etc. The feast began with four male slaves being publicly strangled in honor of the new staff and the hat (men were valued twice as high as women).

When Kunanek died, according to custom, these chiefly regalia were passed on together with the *taion's* status and inheritance to his younger nephew Kaajeex̱dakeen.aa—[*Pereletnyi?*], who brought both the staff and the hat to

Sitka, when he moved there from his old place of residence. When he had a housewarming ceremony in Sitka, he gave an even greater feast in honor of his regalia. Several clans were present at the feast: Chilkat Kanakh-tekety [Gaanaxt-eidí], Hoonah Chakunety [Chookaneidí], Khootznahoo Nushkitany [Wooshkeetaan], etc., not to mention the Sitka Kiks.ádi and L'uknax.ádi. When all the guests assembled, the host, surrounded by his men and dressed in his traditional costume with bear ears on his head (indicating that the bear was the ancestor of his clan), opened the feast with a sacrifice. This was already in the 1850s, when the Russian government had outlawed bloody sacrifices and slavery.[40] Because of that the sacrifice was done in the following way: four slaves or *kalgi* (as they were called) destined to die were placed in front of Kaajeexda-keen.aa. The latter, with the staff raised in his hand, gave a speech in honor of his predecessor Kunanek and other famous ancestors; in conclusion he touched each slave with his staff and let each man hold it, which was the sign that now they were free and could live anywhere, except among the Indians. Such slaves usually went directly to the Russian fort, and those who were war captives were sent home when circumstances allowed.

From that time on, both of these objects were constantly used by the Kaag-waantaan clan on more or less important occasions. Whether somebody died or a new house was built, the festivities organized on these occasions included placing these regalia in a conspicuous place or using them in various important rituals performed by the *taion*.

After the death of Kaajeexdakeen.aa,[41] the *kit-tsakhu* [*Kéet S'áaxw*(?), Killer Whale Hat] and the *ankau-atsakha* [*aankáawu wootsaagáyi*] went to his nephew L'tutakan [Ltoodax'áan]. Before he could take possession of the staff, Ltoodax'áan had to obtain two slaves and set them free by performing the same ritual as his uncle had done. Ltoodax'áan passed the regalia on to his nephew, the son of his sister Shik-sany-kik[?], Kaul'tul'ketl'. The latter also freed a slave, a Kaigani Haida, on this occasion.

When Kaul'tul'ketl' died, there were no direct heirs left. The closest relative and heir of Kaul'tul'ketl' was his aunt Shik-sany-kik[?], a niece of Kunanek—the first owner of these regalia. The only reason she received them was because she had children. Instead of slaves, now difficult to obtain, the famous staff was held above a pile of blankets, later distributed among the guests. Shik-sany-kik had four sons: Kanchukhu [Gooch Ooxú] (Tooth of a Wolf), Tletu [L'eidú], Kokhniku [?], and Kul'kita [Koolkéet'aa]. Shik-sany-kik gave the entire inheritance to her eldest son Gooch Ooxú who, like his mother, gave out blankets worth two slaves. But the new heir did not keep his possessions for too long. He lived after the transfer of Alaska to the Americans and learned how to make his own hoochinoo or home brew. Gooch Ooxú liked to drink and fell a victim to his own passion—drank himself to death. After that the inheritance came into the hands of his two brothers. L'eidú received *aankáawu wootsaagáyi*, and Kokhniku—*Kéet S'áaxw*. Both brothers also died soon thereafter.

Aankáawu wootsaagáyi was inherited by the youngest brother Kul'kita [Koolkéet'aa], the present owner of the staff. On that occasion, following the example of his predecessors, he too gave a feast inviting the Kiks.ádi and the L'uknax.ádi clans and giving them blankets and calico as presents. The hat became the cause of a trial. It was claimed by the *aatlein aankáawu* of the Kaagwaantaan, I. [Ivan] Tlanteech [L.aanteech]. The trial ended in his favor but he had to pay the defense attorney a considerable sum of money. The history of the staff clearly illustrates the importance of clan symbols and family regalia. Among the latter, one must mention the totems or family crests [*famil'nyi gerb*].

The totems are pieces of wood or boards about one and a half feet wide and several *sazhens* long.[42] They are covered with carvings of various animals and birds whose names were once used by famous ancestors. On the very bottom of the board the carving of the original ancestor of the group is located, for instance, a beaver or an otter; its successor is represented above it, e.g., a whale, a bear, or another animal. One might call them the Indian hieroglyphs. Even today, during a feast [potlatch], such totems are still displayed on the front of the *barabora*, while in the old days they remained there permanently.

Generally, in most recent times, fewer and fewer of these regalia remain. Instead of them, nowadays it is not uncommon for a dying *taion* to bequeath to his heir a stack of various written certificates, that he personally or his predecessors had received for various services from the governors and managers of the Russian-American Company, and in later times from the American officers and captains of the men-of-war. The certificates of the first kind, those received from the Russians, are the most highly valued ones.[43] A number of such certificates have been preserved since the days of the governors Hagemeister, Voevodskii, and Etholen. In addition, several silver medals and other decorations have been preserved, e.g., a tsar's caftan [*kaftan*] with a cocked hat, similar to those still awarded to native chieftains in Siberia, a small copper cannon[44] [*ruchnaia pushka*], a similar shield, a double-headed eagle weighing about ten pounds, etc. The silver medals date back to the times of Alexander I.

The Tlingit consider these objects priceless. One could hardly buy them with money. They could only be coaxed with promises of great rewards and honors. American tourists, who visit Sitka in the summer, are as fond of these artifacts as the Indians, and, as almost any citizen of a free country,[45] they like wearing something in their buttonholes. Hence they tried many times to coax these certificates and decorations from the Indians, but none of their attempts have been successful. The Indians' love of dressing up flamboyantly and wearing flashy decorations goes sometimes beyond reason. There is a Tlingit *taion* living in Killisnoo[46]—an aristocrat not without wealth and intelligence. Here is what they tell about him: every time a tourist ship visits his village, he appears in front of the curious Yankees wearing elaborate costumes. Either he is dressed in a general's uniform with numerous stars on his chest, presented to him at various times by the Americans, or as a policeman, or even as a Russian monk wearing a cassock and a cowl. At one time he had a great desire to obtain a bishop's mitre, but so far has not succeeded. Every person he asked for help told him the mitres were worn only by clergy and not laymen. This, however, he could not understand, and instead thought that the reason for the refusal was that his rank was not high enough yet.

Such affection for rank and status is certainly an inherited trait. In the old days, *aankáawu* and especially the *aatlein aankáawu* had tremendous influence on his relatives. Surrounded by a crowd of slaves and captives, they spent times of peace doing nothing but satisfying their vanity by presiding over feasts (of which the Indians are greatly fond), visiting neighboring friendly clans, etc. The best warriors of the clan were always at the disposal of the *taion*, ready at any time to follow their leader to feasts and battles. The leading retainers among them, most often the *taion's* closest relatives, acted as bodyguards and standard-bearers. Usually these positions were filled by his maternal nephews. The *taion* went nowhere without his retinue. Some *taions* used palanquins and carriers just to get into a canoe or to move from one *barabora* to another. Their garments consisted of expensive furs: sables [martens], beavers, ermines, etc.[*47]

At present, as was stated earlier, the status of the *taions* has changed. Not many people are still frightened by their voices. Today almost every Indian fancies himself an *aatlein aankáawu*. In earlier times, under the Russians, some of the friendly chiefs were still honored; they were treated kindly, given presents, and were awarded for their services. The Russians did not interfere in their relations with each other or with members of their clans, except when they themselves asked for it. The American government, however, approached this issue in a very different way. It does not recognize any privileges of the chiefs, considers them equal to other Indians, and in various ways tries to destroy their influence among their neighbors. For this purpose it sometimes selects persons of ordinary rank to serve as policemen in Indian villages.[*48] Despite these and other circumstances of contemporary life, the power of the chiefs is still so strong that it has to be reckoned with, especially in places far removed from the influence of civilization. Nowadays the chiefs are the major adherents to and defenders of the ancient customs and laws. Their success can be measured by the fact that the Indian still adheres strongly to ancient traditions in almost all spheres of social life. This is particularly true of intertribal relationships, family life, beliefs, and various ceremonies.

CHAPTER III

Ideas about Kinship. Relations among Tribes and Clans. Hostage Exchange [Amanatstvo]. Blankets as Units of Value.

Although both Indian tribes, the Wolf and the Raven, call themselves "Tlingit," they treat each other as strangers. Usually a member of the opposite tribe is referred to in his absence as *kunetkanagi* [*guneitkanaaɣí*], i.e., "not one of us," "stranger," while a tribesman is called *akhuni* [*aẋ ẋooní*, sing.] or *akhunki* [*aẋ ẋoonx'í*, plural]— a relative [lit. "(my) friend, (my) relative"].[49] They recognize only the kinship ties based on blood and traced through the maternal line. This is an immutable law, and consequently, an Indian takes a wife from the other tribe, i.e., a man of the Wolf tribe marries a woman of the Raven tribe and vice versa. Within a tribe any female is considered a relative of any male, even when they belong to different clans. Marrying a woman of one's own tribe, even of a different, distinct clan (not related, from our point of view) is considered a terrible disgrace. That is why the word *akhsany* [*aẋ sáni*] i.e., (my) paternal uncle, when used by an Indian, does not [necessarily] indicate close kinship ties, but only certain family relationships. Similarly, men belonging to one of the tribes call those of the other *akh ish* [*aẋ éesh (hás)*], i.e., "our fathers," as, for example, the Kaagwaantaan call the Kiks.ádi men. These brief observations of the Indian ideas about kinship clearly show that for an outsider relationships between relatives are difficult to understand. Nevertheless, these kinship ties are undoubtedly of great importance in the relationships between individuals, tribes, and clans.

One would assume that because of the natural inclination of the Tlingit to feuds and all kinds of intrigue, which in the old days usually resulted in blood-shed and irreconcilable enmity, relationships between the two tribes could only be hostile, and specifically, that one of the two feuding clans would necessarily belong to the Wolf tribe, and the other—to the Raven tribes. In reality, however, the situation is different; conflicts between members of the same tribe are more common, for the following reason: on the one hand, ties between tribesmen, especially those living in different settlements, far from each other, eventually lose their significance, and, on the other, the clans themselves become isolated. Consequently, the distance between some clans of the same tribe is often greater than between clans of different tribes. Thus, as blood relationships lose their effectiveness, marriage ties begin to play a bigger role. Women residing among members of the other tribe are the element counteracting the influence of blood relationships.[50]

A recent feud between two Sitka clans—the Kiks.ádi and the L'uknaẋ.ádi—

39

could be used as an illustration of this phenomenon."[51] Both clans belong to the Raven tribe. The cause of the quarrel was the *khikch* [*xíxch'*] or frog idol."[52] From times immemorial, the Kiks.ádi or Khikhsaty considered the frog to be their ancestor and used its image as the emblem of their clan. The emblem of the L'uknax̱.ádi was the *kiẕiuch-tliuk* [*l'ook*] or [coho] salmon. At the same time, however, their legends preserved clear evidence that not too long ago, not even earlier than the beginning of the nineteenth century, their ancestors revered and possessed the images of both the *l'ook* and the *xíxch'*. The legend speaks about the venerable [*chestnye*] brothers, Yakutat *taions*, who became the ancestors of many of L'uknax̱.ádi *baraboras* and undoubtedly kept the *xíxch'* idol. This legend can be easily explained by the fact that the original ancestor of the clan who gave his name to the L'uknax̱.ádi belonged to the Kiks.ádi clan. Having moved to Yakutat or being the son of a Kiks.ádi woman who married a Yakutat man, he and his descendants led an isolated life and eventually lost all the ties with their relations—the Kiks.ádi, except for their clan idol that they still revered—the *Kootéeyaa Xíxch'* [?"frog crest" or "frog totem"]. His descendants, however, stopped doing that, preferring to revere *l'ook*—the idol of their own original ancestor."[53]

In recent times, the L'uknax̱.ádi moved to Baranof Island in large numbers, multiplied, and formed many well-to-do *baraboras*, and consequently formed a somewhat exaggerated opinion of themselves. Relying in their numerical strength, the L'uknax̱.ádi decided to make the *xíxch'* their emblem, along with the *kiẕiuch* [coho salmon], and thus to demonstrate that they are as ancient as the other Raven clans. The Kiks.ádi call themselves the oldest clan [in Sitka] and the owners of Baranof Island, treating all the other clans of their own and of the opposite tribe as newcomers and vagabonds. However the frog is also the patron of the L'uknax̱.ádi, which makes them equal to the Kiks.ádi and gives them the same right to Baranof Island—the land of the frog. In short, as one of the witnesses of all the troublesome events of their venture put it, the L'uknax̱.ádi daringly decided "to present their noble heraldry to their ignorant kinsmen .... '"[54] As one can see, the affair was carried out with some logic, used by people when they wish to grab something belonging to others.

It was decided to accompany the proclamation of the *xíxch'* as the patron of the L'uknax̱.ádi with solemnity and pomp. According to ancient custom, the *xíxch'* itself was ordered from a craftsman belonging to a distant clan of the opposite moiety. The Kaagwaantaan sided with the L'uknax̱.ádi, because the majority of them are married to members of that clan. In addition they were hoping to gain something from the festivity. There were other, pettier considerations involved as well. Of course, the L'uknax̱.ádi venture did not remain concealed from the Kiks.ádi. Private negotiations failed to produce any results.

Throughout the summer, both clans were in a state of great excitement. The Kiks.ádi threatened to chop up the *xíxch'* of the L'uknax̱.ádi, if the latter dared to display it in the village. Fall and winter—the time when the Indians returned from their fishing and hunting expeditions and when the celebration in honor of the *xíxch'* had to take place—did not cool off the disputants. The festivity itself was supposed to have consisted of the following: a two-*arshin*-long frog, carved crudely from a piece of wood, had to be lifted up to the ridge of the new two-story *barabora* built for the occasion, and displayed for public view, followed by days of celebration, with feasting and distribution of gifts in honor of the great ancestors of the clan. About eight thousand dollars (i.e., fifteen thousand rubles) was spent in preparation for the festivities. Had this happened one hundred or even fifty years before, bloodshed would already have occurred and several human lives would have been sacrificed in honor of the frog-idol. At the present time, however, both parties were hoping for the white man's justice and laws as a last resort. Their faith in these laws was not so strong, however, and consequently both parties headed by their *taions* quickly hired defense attorneys, spending another large sum of money. This time, however, the affair ended most unexpectedly with the death of a L'uknax.ádi *taion* and the fact that "the frog had to be moved to the firewood stack to be chopped into splinters...[?]" But it is uncertain whether the frog has in fact been moved to the woodstack and passions have calmed. For somebody who knows the Indian nature intimately, it is hard to believe that this dispute and venture have ended forever.

During all the trouble, accompanied by nightly meetings on both sides, visits to American officials, and quarrels, the Kaagwaantaan and other clans of the same tribe, as was mentioned earlier, had to remain on friendly terms with the L'uknax.ádi. They played that role mainly because their leading *taions* are married to Kaagwaantaan women. Thus marriage ties overrode tribal ties and blood relationships. Women served as a peacemaking link.

The same thing is repeated in many other cases. In the old days, when every quarrel was accompanied by bloodshed, women played this role more actively. They usually stood bravely with their quarreling husbands, on the one side, and brothers and fathers on the other.*[55] In cases of hostility between two clans of the same tribe, (as in the case just mentioned), being members of the opposite tribe, they played a pacifying role, and in a way served as arbitrators.

In some cases, women overstepped the limits [of propriety]. During bloody battles, the women were concerned with both the fate of their husbands as well as their blood relatives. This probably could explain why most of the fierce and bloody confrontations between Indian men ended in even bloodier fights between women. When their peaceful mediations failed, the women initiated their own fighting using knives. This usually signaled the men to end their own battle, and at that point they became spectators of the peculiar fighting between their women. Legends describe the most incredible battles of this kind. For some reason they always took place in the water, on shore, or in the river

41

dividing the two hostile camps. Half-naked women, with their hair loose and water reaching up to their breasts, fought with knives. Fierceness reached extreme proportions on both sides. While male warriors, protected by armor from head to toe, used certain tactics and tricks in battle, allowing them to escape with only light wounds, women cut each other up, wounding unprotected bodies. The scene of such a battle, where every gaping wound colored the water with streaming blood and where the falling warriors found their end on the bottom of the sea or the river, was so inhumanly violent, that even the wild male warriors were moved and re-entered the battle, just to put an end to the bloodshed.[56]

Quarrels and fights between Indians of the same village, related to each other in one way or another, were usually carried out and ended in this manner. However, if warfare began between two different clans of different and distant villages, then the warriors of one clan outfitted several war canoes, approached the enemy village, and, with a terrible noise, attacked the enemy in the dead of night. Such attacks were aimed at capturing as many prisoners as possible. Women and children were not killed in the course of battle. Among the Indians, to attack a woman and fight with her is considered a great shame. Such raids usually ended in either a total victory of the attackers and the capture of numerous prisoners, or, if the attackers were unable to hold their positions and caused only some damage, they were then pursued during their retreat, which resulted in frequent naval battles. In most cases captives were ransomed. For that purpose warring clans made peace, exchanged captives, or traded purchased slaves for those that had been captured from them by the enemy.

To strengthen peace and friendship, *amanatstvo* or an exchange of hostages was used. Usually children of *taions* were taken as hostages and treated with great respect. *Amanatstvo* was also popular among the Russians, when they had to pacify the Alaskans. This was the only way Baranov was able to force Indian tribes to maintain friendly relations with him, threatening to kill hostages in case of hostile actions.

However, sometimes peace between two clans could not be established for a very long time, especially when they lived far away from each other. Occasionally, hostilities dragged on for tens or even hundreds of years. Such, for example, was the feud between the Sitka Kaagwaantaan and the Stakhin [Stikine] Indians. Here is the history of this conflict. About fifty or more years ago, there was a quarrel between the Stikines and the Kaagwaantaan, which ended in a truce. Despite that the Kaagwaantaan believed that they had not been avenged and were only waiting for an opportunity to do so; and soon they had one. When the Stikines came to visit the Kaagwaantaan, they were received with the usual ceremonies and then invited to the largest *barabora* for a feast. Suspecting nothing, the unarmed guests took their seats around a table. This was, however, the moment chosen by the Kaagwaantaan for avenging their old wrongs. While performing the war dance in honor of the newly arrived guests, they filled the whole *barabora* and, upon a special signal, carried out an all-out slaughter. They say that the decapitated bodies of the Stikines covered the whole beach of the village. When the remains of the dead were transported to the so-called Japonski Island (where even in present times many human bones lie scattered), the enemy heads alone filled several huge canoes.*[57]

Since this massacre, the Stikines and the Kaagwaantaan have remained worst enemies, even into the present time. The Stikines consider themselves greatly "indebted" and use every available opportunity to "pay" this "debt." Since the fear of being brought to court prevents the Sitkines from open revenge, they make sudden attacks on their enemies when the latter approach their shores during marine hunting and fishing. They say that there have already been quite a few cases of Kaagwaantaan disappearing without a trace.

Such vindictiveness and retentive memory are simply manifestations of the ancient custom of blood revenge. It owes its stability to the fact that the Tlingit do not trust or respect the laws of the white people, because the latter can be bribed and also, to some extent, because the Indians do not understand them. Hence they still believe in the good quality, so to speak, of their customary bloody law. The fear of having to pay with one's own life for that of another, blood for blood, and wound for wound, can cool the hottest head and stop the hand of the most ferocious murderer.

Another manifestation of the same law in Indian social life is a peculiar custom of paying for everything—a wound, an insult, or harm, even that which is done inadvertently. This custom developed in the most recent times under the influence of the new conditions of life, which did not allow the Indian to carry out the ancient custom of blood revenge in its entirety; this deficiency was compensated to some extent by payment. To characterize this phenomenon fully one cannot simply use the word "payment" but must refer to it as a "payment in blankets .... " This is a rather curious system of making payments, which is also closely connected with the question of "units of value."

In the days of old the Tlingit had no notion of metal money or paper currency. To some extent, slaves or *kalgi*, later on animal skins, and even later *siukli* [dentalium shells] were used as units of value similar to sable and marten furs among the Russians and other peoples several centuries ago.[3]*[58]

The same things, that is, slaves, furs, and *siukli*, constituted the total wealth of an Indian. However, as the Indians became better and better acquainted with the Europeans, wealth began to be accumulated in a different way. The pressure from the European civilization eliminated slavery along with primitive tribal warfare, while the *siukli* themselves lost their value and were replaced by blankets. The reason that blankets, and not any other item, became the unit of value can probably be explained by the fact that they became one of the most useful things in native daily life. An Indian cannot do without a blanket, which is used not only for sleeping but at all times. In this respect the Indian resembles the people of the ancient world. For public appearances, Romans and Greeks draped themselves in togas, Indians wear blankets. They are always worn for festivities and various kinds of gatherings, even by those among them who usually dress in European clothing. For that purpose alone one had to have a considerable supply of blankets. Some of the *taions* own thousands of them, with a great variety of colors and value. The value of an ordinary American blanket is between two and five dollars. English ones are favored over American. The most highly valued blankets are black [dark blue] trimmed with red [woolen] cloth and have pearl buttons sewn on the trimming [i.e., on the dark background next to the inner edges of the red stripes]. They are called *nakhen* [*naaxein*].*[59] Every *taion* has to have such a blanket for special festive occasions. The most expensive ones—the so-called Chilkat blankets—are made by the Indians themselves out of white mountain goat wool. They are always woven, or rather, knitted, out of threads of different colors. The latter are used to represent various images similar to those carved on totem poles. The price of a single Chilkat blanket sometimes reaches above 100 dollars. Such blankets are in greatest demand among tourists.

Blankets play the role of money among the Tlingit. They are used in all of the deals and transactions between natives, so that the payments themselves acquire a special, ceremonial character. As has been noted above, there are countless reasons for making payments. Besides well-known motives, a significant role in the development of this payment system is taken by an inborn affection for an easy profit involving speculation and risk. This trait seems to be even more strongly developed among the Indians than among the Jews. Although the former have no signs for numbers and do not keep written records, but use [tally] sticks tied into bundles for counting, they are, nevertheless, great mathematicians whom it is absolutely impossible to cheat. Every fall, when they return to their villages from different places, numerous trials, countings, and payments in blankets begin, with such intricate details that an unaccustomed person would get totally confused.

There are all sorts of reasons for making payments: an accidental injury of one person by another, a disease acquired by a husband from his wife, a fight among children resulting in cuts. An injured or insulted person summons all of his kin, and if he is a nobleman his entire clan, and distributes blankets among them as presents. This means that he is appealing to his clan for help and is sharing his injury among all of its members, who are thus obliged to defend the victim's honor. And so the whole *barabora*, and sometimes the whole clan, are up in arms and are seeking retribution for the injury of their member. The adverse party anticipates this and appeals to its own relatives for the injury. If they do not wish to act that way, they must expect at any time an insult twice or three times greater than the original one.*[60] Having made the payment, however, they do not lose hope of receiving their property back, even with interest, since they now have the right of revenge, and all that is needed is a cause for mobilizing their own kin. And so it goes without end.[61]

There are specialists among the Indians, similar to lawyers, who constantly create causes for payments. Besides that, there are distributions of inheritance, potlatches on the occasion of building and dedicating new *baraboras*, deaths of clan members, reception of guests from other villages, gifts to the shaman and fines paid to American courts. Yes, strange as it may seem, judges even recently were actually paid in blankets. Thus poor blankets change hands and travel all over the village. There are days in the life of the Sitka Indians when they are seen constantly dragging blankets back and forth—single ones, piles, and chests-full. In further discussions, we shall still encounter the notorious blankets once more.

CHAPTER IV

Marriage and Family Life. Divorces. Remarriage of the Widowed. Polygamy. Children's Upbringing During the First Year.

Among the Tlingit, there is a story or rather a romantic legend about a brother's carnal love for his sister and a cruel punishment inflicted upon them by fate. The poor girl, pursued by her brother's shadow[?] or chasing it unsuccessfully herself, was so tormented by love that she finally threw herself into the sea from a high cliff. Since then the brother hears her voice calling him for help, but cannot approach her. This legend serves as a kind of dogma, which is the basis of the Indian custom of marrying only members of the opposite tribe [moiety].*[62]

In most cases, the groom selects his bride by following the instructions of his senior kin, although he does not remain completely indifferent to the choice. Usually, if the groom is a young lad and the bride is a maiden, romantic stories are not uncommon. In this case the Indians resemble our Gypsies—the free children of the Bessarabian steppes. It is not easy to marry off an Indian girl against her will. Her love is whimsical and sometimes stubborn. Tlingit stories about love are full of wonderful exploits. Indians believe in spells, charms, black magic, and love formulas and incantations; they also believe in the existence of certain roots of mysterious plants and herbs which can be used to win the most indifferent heart. However, in most cases reality and tradition play their crucial role, so that no matter how romantic a story serves as the basis of the prospective marriage, the groom usually has to earn the right to take his bride. For that purpose he moves into her *barabora* and serves her parents. Everything obtained by him through hunting and other activities has to be presented to the bride's father and mother. The groom is also expected to show certain modesty and respect toward the elders and his superiors. In this case the Tlingit follow an ancient proverb which says that the one who has not learned how to obey, would not be able to command. There is no definite time period for such a trial—sometimes it lasts for a year, sometimes for two. The usual marriageable age for men is seventeen or eighteen, and for women—the time of the first [menstrual] period, i.e., fifteen or sixteen.

When a Tlingit girl reaches full maturity and enters the ranks of brides, certain rituals are performed. First of all, before she is recognized as a bride, the girl is separated from her entire family and placed into a dark corner partitioned off by canvas or a screen (in the old days a separate tent was used). This is done so that nobody could see her, while she could neither speak to anybody, nor touch anybody or anything. She had to remain in this state for several months.

47

This custom is strictly observed by the Indians. There has not been a single case of an Indian woman marrying without undergoing this ordeal and observing this taboo.

This custom persists among the Indians probably because of their ideas about female impurity, if one could use this expression to refer to the usual female menstrual periods. The Indians believe that even animals avoid this impurity and fear nothing as much as women. Because of that, when a man prepares for a hunting expedition, especially for such a noble animal as sea otter, he stops all [sexual] relations with his wife. If a hunter is unsuccessful, if the animal he is pursuing runs away, it is a sure sign that his wife is breaking the vows of fidelity and not observing the taboo. In the opinion of the Indians, numerous misfortunes result from the non-observance of the custom of requiring a girl to spend several months in confinement upon reaching puberty. Fish do not come near the shore at the usual time, so that people fail to store food and consequently starve in the winter; animals are not killed; violent storms rage on the sea, many people drown, and so on. All of this is caused by the violators of the above-mentioned custom. Therefore, if an Indian suffers a misfortune during a storm, and especially if someone drowns, relatives of the victim immediately find the culprit and receive a payment from her parents in the form of a pile or several chests full of blankets and other valuables. The latter practice has a considerable influence on the fact that this rather primitive custom is still adhered to by the Indians of today.

The Tlingit do not have any special marriage ceremonies, except for the exchange of presents between the parents of the groom and those of the bride, as well as a feast.[*63] In most cases Indian marriages involve partners of different ages; it is unusual for a young Indian man to marry a young woman. Usually, either the husband is a young lad while the wife is an old woman, or the wife has just reached puberty and the husband is an old man. Here is why it happens. The Tlingit never gives anything to anybody for free. Having given something to somebody, he considers that person to be his debtor for life. The same reasoning operates in marriage. When an Indian becomes a widower and loses his wife, whom he had once obtained by working for her parents and giving them presents, he cherishes the hope that the relatives of the deceased will give him a new wife. Of course new presents and some other expenses are inevitable, but the total cost of dealing with an indebted *barabora* is far smaller than if the groom decided to establish affinal ties with another *barabora*, which owes him nothing.

As a result of such calculations, a widower often receives a younger sister or a niece [sister's daughter] of his deceased wife. Sometimes a very old man receives one of the young girls of the same *barabora* to which his first wife had belonged. In that case an additional fact is taken into consideration—if there are any surviving children, the new mother, belonging to the same family as the deceased and being a close blood relative of the orphans, would love them and take good care of them. Under these circumstances, elderly widows act in exactly the same way. The latter, when they need to obtain a young husband, are often even more generous than old men.

Of course, such customs have a bad influence on family life and contribute significantly to the degeneration of the Indians. The latter understand this themselves and, in order to paralyze and somehow weaken the unnatural character and harm of such marriages, allow bigamy and sometimes even polgamy. The acquisition of the second wife no longer requires any special labor or expenses. The task of obtaining her is the responsibility of the first one. Usually bigamy takes place in those cases when the husband is young while the wife is fairly old. In that case, by obtaining another young wife for her husband, the old wife gives him a surprise of sorts, while providing herself with a loyal and obedient helper in household chores. Not uncommon are the cases when the second wife is the daughter of the old one, but from a different husband, or her close [matrilineal] relative. In case the old wife has neither a daughter nor a female relative whom she can eventually offer to her husband as a second wife, she then tries ahead of time to adopt a girl whom she raises sometimes for many years. In these cases the husband himself usually stays away. It is a great shame for an Indian male to be interested and involved in such intimate affairs; this is the business of women only. Of course, secretly the husband is as interested in his family affairs as his wife. But such is their manner of appropriate behavior, which demands that a man-warrior maintains complete tranquility and outward composure in all of the complicated circumstances of life.

An Indian rarely has more than two wives. If there were any occurrences of a man having three or more wives, those always date back to the savage stage in their history and in most cases the third or the fourth wife was not a free woman, but a captive or a slave of an aristocratic, *taion* background. But even in those cases the role of the old wife did not change. She was the only one to have the right under special circumstances to give the captive woman the honor to be a wife equal to herself. However, children of such wives could never enjoy the full rights of inheritance. At the present time, one rarely hears about bigamy, not to mention polygamy; if such cases occasionally occur, they are kept a great secret from the whites.

Divorces are not uncommon among the Indians. In the past, divorces were rare, since all the Tlingit used to live according to their ancient customs or were married in the Orthodox Church, which is rather skeptical about divorces. Nowadays, however, with the help of the Presbyterian missionaries, American civil practices, including civil marriages contracted in the judge's office, are being implanted among the Indians who, following the example of their enlighteners, are becoming very fond of divorces.[*64]

In the family life, women enjoy considerable freedom and have their special rights. A Tlingit man's wife is neither his slave nor simply a worker, as is common among savages. She is more in command in the house and family matters than her husband. While the husband is busy with public affairs and hunting far away from his *barabora*, the wife is in total control of the house and the family. She is in charge of all the property and food supplies of an Indian household, simple as they are. She also takes over everything obtained by the head of the family during hunting and fishing expeditions. As mistresses of their houses Indian women are very energetic and efficient.

Long Alaskan winters, when it is difficult and at times simply impossible to go out hunting, demand large food supplies. Also needed are warm clothing, waterproof footwear, and so forth. Storing up all of this is the women's responsibility. They skillfully prepare the meat of various game animals which their husbands provide, so that nothing is wasted. They know how to dry and dry-cure all kinds of fish, turning it into *iukola* which serves the Indians as bread all year round; they also prepare herring roe, smoked bear meat, *iamanina* (mountain goat meat); render whale and seal grease and store up a variety of berries and roots in it. From deer and seal skins they prepare soft waterproof tanned hides used for making clothing, moccasins, bags, etc.

Tlingit women spend the long winter evenings making [i]shkats or baskets of various sizes and shapes. They are made of thin tree roots painted with different colors. In the past, they served the Indians as kitchen dishes, which could be used for boiling water and preparing meals. The art of making baskets has been brought to perfection by these Indians. The art of embroidery flourishes among them as well. One of the favorite types of embroidery involves the use of beads and pearl buttons on cloth and tanned hide. Elegant little things, such as purses, slippers, etc., are eagerly bought up by tourists-travellers visiting Alaska. This causes Tlingit women in some places to engage in a special trade—preparing these objects for the summer tourist season. It is not uncommon for a single woman to prepare many artifacts during the winter and to sell them during the summer for as much as 300 dollars. Resourcefulness and prudence are the natural qualitites of an Indian woman, developed since long ago when the Indians did not know the easy ways of obtaining clothing and everything necessary in daily life for money from the merchant's store, and when everything had to be made with their own hands. Sometimes their thrift becomes stinginess. It seems incomprehensible that the latter would coexist with wastefulness. Very often great wealth accumulated through extraordinary efforts, labor, and thrift is all spent by the Tlingit in one or two days of feasting and distributing gifts among guests. This phenomenon can only be explained by tremendous vanity forming part of their character."[65]

The upbringing of children was and still is the most sacred and inalienable right of the Tlingit woman. Compared to the family life of other peoples, this right is strengthened among them by law which makes the children the blood relatives only of the mother and her own [matrilineal] kin. Hence men never interfere in this domain of the rights of the woman as a mother and educator. Boys leave the guardianship of the mother rather early. At about the age of twelve or thirteen they submit to the authority not so much of their father, but their maternal uncle from whom they learn everything a good Tlingit man has to know. Girls, however, remain under the mother's supervision until the very time of their marriage. In the olden days, according to the Indians, the upbringing of women was very strict. Although young girls were not banned from the company of men and were not kept in separate quarters and confinement, as was done in the past among some peoples, they were strongly restricted in their relations with men by the special demands and rules of the Indian etiquette. For example, it was considered a great shame for a girl to look straight into a man's face, even if he was a close relative. The mother bears all the responsibility for her daughter's behavior prior to marriage. Consequently mothers receive the best gift when their daughters are married and play the decisive role in the family councils dealing with marriage issues.

In general Tlingit women are good, loving mothers. From the moment when a new little creature enters the world and finds itself in a sort of a nest made of fluffy forest mosses, especially prepared for the occasion (as a sign of the fact that their god—Yéil—was born in a raven's nest made of moss), the mother never parts with it and rarely keeps the child away from her arms. To make carrying the baby easier and its sleep more comfortable, the whole body is tied to a small board and placed in a small basket which has the form of half an egg and a length equal to that of the baby's body. The latter is also tied to this basket and in this manner is carried in the mother's arms or, during travel, on her back. In this respect the Alaskan Indians strongly resemble those of the mainland that I have seen in the states of Wyoming and Nebraska. Until the age of one or sometimes longer Indian mothers feed their infants only with their own milk.

These are the general features of the Tlingit family life. Some of its specific details and minute characteristics (which are, however, gradually disappearing as the Indians become acquainted with whites), resemble the customs of the patriarchal-Biblical times. Observations of the reality, which are so difficult to recreate fully on paper, could carry the observer's imagination far back into past centuries, to the beginning of the history of mankind, when almost the same forms of family life, which only recently still characterized Indian life, were inspired and imbued with the spirit that had created them.

CHAPTER V

Ancient Religions of the Indians. Traces of True Worship.

When the Russians discovered Alaska and for the first time met with the Tlingit—the inhabitants of its southeastern part—they found them in the last stage of savagery; as far as their religion was concerned, they were in a stage usually called fetishism, in its shamanistic form. Having lost the clear notions of the Deity, their coarsened minds became incapable of conceiving of God as the creator and the Providence of the universe. The Indian transferred divine characteristics to anthropomorphic beings, half-humans, half-animals. Later on, as the notion of the Deity was becoming more and more obscure, these characteristics were attributed to some of the natural phenomena surrounding him, either threatening or clearly beneficial, as well as to some animate and inanimate objects. One Great Spirit worshipped by all of mankind was replaced by numerous independent spirits perceived by the Indian as controlling natural phenomena and the destiny of every individual human being. At first, the Indian saw these spirits only in majestic and outstanding natural phenomena, but later on he populated canyons, forests, valleys, and mountains with them, seeing manifestations of their power not only in animals but in trees, stones, and any other objects. Subsequently finding great similarity between spiritual attributes of man and animals, he identified the nature of the spirits. He began populating with the spirits of the dead not only certain selected places (where they supposedly dwelled), but animals as well. Thus an Indian cult of venerating the spirits of the dead and the belief in the transmigration of souls were created.

This, however, was not the end of his religious degradation. It continued with his spiritual degeneration. The materialization of the idea of the Deity developed in accordance with the gradual obscuring of the God-revealed [*bogootkrovennye*] truths and the hardening of the human minds and hearts. As more spirits were created by the savage's imagination, each of them was left with fewer divine qualities and powers. In the whole pantheon of spirits, each one was given its own specific domain of activity and a certain degree of power. Yet most of them were considered to be superior to man by their nature, so that almost every spirit had an opportunity to influence him.

However, this development did not leave man completely helpless. Although he did invent spirits and constantly placed himself in total dependence on them, it was not absolute. He also invented ways of influencing spirits—placating some so that they would help him in his unequal struggle against the elements, wild animals, and unfriendly tribes, and propitiating others so that they would not harm him. Every human being cannot learn how to use all of this knowledge, and besides, this is totally unnecessary. If all people could influence spirits, the latter would have been in trouble. Justice demanded that spirits would not be disparaged too much for the benefit of man himself. Hence the skills and the right to communicate with the world of spirits were appropriated by certain selected persons that the Indians called íxt', i.e., medicine man, prophet, shaman. Further materialization of Indian beliefs stopped at the stage of shamanism.

With these features, Tlingit Indian beliefs, particularly in this last stage of degeneration, have much in common with the shamanistic religion of Siberian natives, i.e., Chukchees, Tungus, etc. This fact is the most convincing argument for the common place of origin of the Alaskan Indian religion and all other religions [?], i.e., the Asiatic continent. The process itself, which accompanied the distortion of truth and the transition from the true knowledge of God to crude heathenism, supports this idea and is the same as the development of other heathen religions.

This was the case with the Egyptian, Greek, Chinese, and other mythologies. From the belief in the existence of the Great Spirit, people shifted to the belief in spirits and later on in visible natural phenomena and objects identified with the action and power of spirits. Subsequently the force of habit led to the idolization of the object itself. Despite all this, traces of ancient beliefs—always superior to the later ones—remain. Thus, the Ancient Egyptian beliefs of the times of King Minos turned later on into primitive superstitions and worship of thousands of various reptiles and animals. Greek deities of Hesiod's time, having multiplied on Olympus, acquired anthropomorphic form and character with all of the human flaws and vices. The Chinese, having abandoned the worship of Shang Ti—the Supreme ruler or the ruler of the Sky, worshipped the single God Ti or Tea, but subsequently divided into three camps. Some of them, the so-called Confucianists, give offerings to the sky and worship numerous spirits and souls of the dead; others profess Taoism—the religion of the incantations; and others follow crude Buddhism. As a matter of fact, all of these peoples have undergone the same psychic process of the materialization of the idea of the Deity, with the only difference being that some of them departed further from the Biblical background than others.

According to their characteristic features and the time of origin, all Tlingit beliefs can be divided into several categories. The first one is constituted by the most ancient beliefs about Kanuk [Ganook, petrel] and other anthropomorphic gods and titans similar to him; then there are also legends about El [Yéil, raven], Agishanuku [Haayeeshaanák'u], Khetl [Xeitl], and others. One could frequently hear echoes of Biblical narratives in the stories about these gods and semi-gods. The second category consists of ideas about the souls of the dead and their life in the other world, as well as beliefs in an endless multitude of different spirits closely linked to various rituals, especially the mortuary ones. This category of ideas and beliefs serves, in a way, as a transition to primitive shamanism, which constitutes the third and the last category and represents primitive belief in magic and witchcraft.

CHAPTER VI

Indian Deities: Dikée Aankáawu, Ganook and Yéil. Myths about Them.

The idea of the Supreme Being has been poorly preserved in the people's memory. Although there is a Tlingit word Dikée Aankáawu[66] meaning the Superior Chief, Ruler of the Sky, the Indian has a vague notion about this ruler of the Sky, the nature of his domain and of those ruled by him. He only knows that this being lives somewhere on top of a mountain where a light, cool breeze blows, green grass always grows, and sky-blue flowers bloom, and where an eternal silence reigns, undisturbed even by the sound of the surf. Except for this the Indian knows nothing about the Ruler of the Sky. He does not consider Dikée Aankáawu to be either the Creator or the Providence of the world. All of these notions are transferred to other gods such as Ganook, Yéil, Haay-eeshaanák'u, Xeitl.[67]

Ganook or the Sitting One[4],[68] is considered to be the senior and the most ancient of all the Indian deities. Myths attribute to Ganook the original power over the whole earth. He existed even before the world acquired its present appearance. His power, shared with several titans[69] similar to him, extended over everything. When Ganook reigned, there were no stars in the sky, no moon, no sun; it seems that even on earth itself (owned by Ganook and the titans) there was no order, i.e., no seas, rivers, plants, or animals. Human beings knew nothing about these phenomena and owned none of them. The heavenly bodies were kept in boxes by some old titan. The water was kept in a certain well on an isolated island by Ganook himself. Fish, birds and animals were also locked up and kept somewhere on that island. Myths are very uncertain about the mode of human existence at that time. The world and mankind itself were led out of their miserable condition by Yéil. According to Indian myths, he is a god-benefactor, similar to Brahmanist Visvakarman.[70]

Here is what Tlingit myths tell about Ganook, Yéil, and their relationships. Their first encounter occurred under the following circumstances. Once upon a time, Ganook travelling in a canoe met Yéil, also in a canoe, and asked him: "How long have you been living in the world?"

Yéil answered that he was born when the earth had not yet been moved to its present location.[71]

"Oh", replied Ganook. Then Yéil asked him:

"So, and how long have you been living in the world?"

"Since the time when the liver has come up from underneath."[72]

"Yes", said Yéil, "you are older than I am."

Whereas Ganook, according to myths, is an anthropomorphic being, Yéil is endowed with the ability to change his appearance constantly. Sometimes he is simply a raven whose name he is bearing, sometimes a human being, and sometimes he acts as an invisible spirit. His major pastime is changing from one appearance to another. He is a loyal and eternal friend of human beings, although he sometimes does not mind punishing them when their disobedience or mockery anger him.

The following story is told about Yéil's appearance on earth in human form. Once upon a time, there was no light, day, or night on earth yet. Mankind lived in darkness, knowing or owning nothing. During that time, in the land of Nass [River], there lived one great chief, the owner of this world, named Nashakietl [Naasshagiyéil (lit. "Raven at the head of Nass")][73] who possessed the sun, the moon, and the stars. In addition, he had a beautiful daughter. The heavenly bodies were kept in boxes. There were no other men in the land of Nass, except for Naasshagiyéil's grandfather, a decrepit old man named Kakakhkanuk.[*74] Yéil wished to become human by being born through this particular girl. But the strict father, extremely fond of his daughter, watched everything she did very carefully, even what she ate and drank. Yéil saw that it would be very hard for him to enter the girl's body by ordinary means. And so, in his usual manner, he resorted to trickery. He turned into a tiny seed and stuck to the vessel of water when the girl was drinking from it. Thus he was swallowed by her and, as a result, she became pregnant. When the time came for Yéil to be born, the girl's father ordered a comfortable place to be prepared for her. Beaver and other valuable furs were spread everywhere to make her place of delivery comfortable and soft. But the parturient could not give birth until, following the advice of an old woman, she was placed outside the *barabora* in the forest, underneath a shady tree. Her bed was made of soft forest moss similar to that used by ravens in making nests. After that Yéil immediately emerged into the world. Thus, at the very moment of his birth Yéil revealed his raven's habits. Imitating Yéil, Indian women now give birth on a bed of moss.

Neither the grandfather, nor the mother, nor anybody else suspected that the newborn infant was not an ordinary human being but a god. The grandfather loved his grandson very much and spoiled him. Although the grandson was very naughty, all his caprices were immediately satisfied. From the first days of his life, Yéil began to show his wild and willful temper. Once he was crying so bitterly that nothing could console him. Whatever he was given was thrown away, while the child persistently tried to reach the boxes containing the heavenly bodies. The grandfather took pity on his grandson and allowed one box to be given to him. The crybaby was consoled, became happy, and immediately ran away to play. Seeing that nobody was watching, he opened the box with the stars. They soared and remained in the sky. From then they began to shine from above, while the box remained empty.

When the grandfather found out about his grandson's act, he regretted the loss of his treasure but did not get angry at the child, since he did not suspect even for a minute that it had been a trick. In the meantime the grandson was coveting the other two boxes and was soon able to get his hands on them. Similar to the stars, he let the moon out of the second box. For a long time the grandfather would not trust him with the third box containing the sun, so that Yéil became ill from crying, disappointment, and refusal to eat. Watching his grandson's behavior, the grandfather was bewildered and perplexed by his stubbornness. The great-grandfather Kakakhkanuk also came to take a look at the child and became very displeased with him. "He even has raven's eyes—nothing good will come of him," said the old man . . . . This derisive but truthful observation infuriated Yéil. He did finally receive the box, but on condition that he would not try to open it. This was all Yéil needed. As soon as he left the *barabora*, he immediately turned into a raven, flew up and disappeared with the box. He landed at the place where people were living. Hearing their voices in the darkness he approached them.

"Who are you and would you like to have light?" he asked them. They told him he was a liar and that only Yéil could give light. To convince the unbelievers Yéil opened the lid of the box and immediately the sun appeared in the sky in all of its shining glory. But the people could not stand its brightness and ran away in all directions, some to the forest, some to the mountains, some to the water, etc. That is why there are so many anthropomorphic animals both in the forest and the water, for example, beavers, land otters, bears, etc.[*75]

This is the story of how Yéil obtained the heavenly bodies for mankind—the stars, the moon, the sun. Such was his first visit to earth in human form. Subsequently he came back many times in the same appearance. His second visit occurred under the following circumstances. Deep in the *chaga* [giant spruce] forest lived one famous *taion* or chief skilled in building canoes. Nobody built such boats at that time for two reasons: first of all, because the *chaga* tree used to grow only in this man's domain, and, secondly, because nobody knew how. The chief lived in isolation, far away from any human habitation. He had a wife whom he loved and jealously guarded. She had eight very pretty little birds of golden color, similar to humming-birds, called *kóon* [flicker]. The birds always remained near her, four of them sitting on each side of her chest. The only time they flew away from her, was when the woman favored somebody in her husband's absence. To prevent such occurrences her jealous husband would lock her up in a box whenever he had to go to work.

He also had a sister named Kitkukhinsi [?], i.e., daughter of a killer whale. The latter had eight sons from someone, but the jealous and suspicious uncle killed all of them. Some of them he drowned by taking them out to sea in his canoe and pushing them overboard; others were locked up in a hollowed log, which he burned out for making canoes. Thus all eight of them were destroyed one after another. The mother cried bitterly, mourning the loss of her children. Finally she decided to run away from her cruel brother. She found an isolated place and settled there choosing heron or *tliak* [*láx'*] as her husband. Once, while catching fish, the heron found a black pebble on the bottom of the sea near the shore. He brought it home and showed it to Kitkukhinsi who swallowed it and soon became pregnant.[5]

When the child was born, the mother was very happy, thinking that he was an ordinary human being. But it was Yéil himself. From very early on he began to show unusual talents. From the age of seven, he already went hunting and shot arrows with great accuracy, using the bow made by his mother. Once he shot so many tiny little birds that his mother was able to make a parka out of their skins. To store the game he had shot, Yéil built a small hut [*baraborka*, a small *barabora*], where he, as a true hunter, spent most of his time.

Once he was sitting in his hut and saw a big bird land very close to the entrance to his *barabora*. It was called *kukgatuli*, [*gus'yadóoli*, sandpiper] similar to magpie, with a tail and a very long, thin beak hard as steel. Yéil killed the bird, skinned it in the usual manner, and dried it. One time he decided to try this skin on. As soon as he put it on, he felt an ability to fly like a bird. Without thinking twice, he soared and flew up so high that the beak hit the sky and got stuck in a cloud. There Yéil was hanging, until he barely managed to pull his beak out. When Yéil returned to his *barabora*, he took off the magic skin and hung it up in a special separate place. Soon thereafter he managed to kill a large duck out on the water; he skinned it and asked his mother to try it on. Thus she acquired an ability to swim in the sea.

When Yéil grew up, his mother told him about all the cruelties of his uncle. Yéil became indignant and decided to teach him a lesson immediately. He went to his house and, not having found him at home, opened the box where his uncle's wife was kept whenever her husband was away. The birds called *kóon* immediately flew away from her. When the uncle returned after a day of work, he found Yéil in his *barabora* and, seeing the confusion, became very angry. But Yéil was not a bit embarrassed. The uncle then invited Yéil to follow him to the beach [*laida*], put him in a canoe, took him to the place where he used to hollow logs, and locked him up in one of those logs. He thought this would kill Yéil, just as it had destroyed his brothers. But this was nothing for Yéil. He broke the log and, before the uncle reached his own house, Yéil had already been sitting there for a long time.[6]

After that the uncle had to think very hard how to punish and destroy Yéil. He could not think of anything better than to cause a great flood all over the world. In this blind rage against his nephew, the uncle made the water cover all of the dry land. Once again, however, he proved to be wrong. As soon as the water began covering the land and rising higher and higher, Yéil hurried to his own *barabora*. He told his mother to wear the duck skin, while he put on the skin of the *gus'yadóoli*. His mother turned into a sea duck and began swimming on the surface of the water. Yéil, in the meantime, soared to the clouds and stuck his beak into the sky as he had done before. There he hung until the flood had stopped and almost all of the water covering the earth had dried up. Before it happened, the water was reaching all the way up to the clouds, so that even Yéil's tail and wings got wet . . . .

When the flood was over, Yéil fell down at the place of the sunset, not directly on land but still on the water. He landed on some seaweed [*morskaia kapusta*] and from there a sea otter carried him ashore. According to another version, he came down to earth near his uncle's house. To take vengeance on his uncle, Yéil gathered *chaga* chips and cones into his long beak and flew toward the place where people where living. He scattered those cones and chips along the way and, wherever they fell, a *chaga* tree sprang up. Yéil taught mankind how to build canoes out of that tree, which until then had been built only by his uncle. Yéil knew that man cannot live without a canoe.[76]

As the myth tells us, Yéil himself was very fond of going out in a canoe. He was especially eager to visit Ganook who lived on a bare, treeless island called Tekinum [Deikee Noow]. This was the only place where one could find fresh drinking water . . . . It was kept in a stone well and some Indians still show the remains of this well on one of the islands located very close to the southernmost end of Baranof Island, near Cape Ommaney or Shagliutu [Sheey Lutú]. Here, fresh water was kept in a square stone box covered with a heavy lid. The well was continuously guarded by Ganook himself. And that was the island Yéil set out to visit.

The meeting between Yéil and Ganook and the nature of their conversation have already been described earlier. The story goes on to tell how, during that conversation, Ganook, probably wishing to show his power and superiority over Yéil, took off his hat and placed it behind himself. This caused such a thick fog to cover the surface of the sea, that one could not see the bow of the canoe from its stern. At that moment Ganook purposely moved his boat away from Yéil, leaving him alone. Unable to see anything, Yéil wandered around for a long time and finally began calling Ganook: *"Ax káani! Ax káani!"* [my brother-in-law].

But Ganook kept silent. Yéil tried to go this way and that way but had no idea what the right direction was. He kept calling his companion for a long time but received no answer. Finally he began to cry and implore Ganook to come back to him. Then Ganook came up closely and asked him, "Well, what is the matter? Why are you crying?" Having said that, he put his hat back on and the fog disappeared immediately. Then Yéil told him, "Well, *ax káani*, you are stronger than I am."

Following that Ganook invited Yéil to visit him on the above mentioned island Deikee Noow. Among other treats, Ganook offered his guest some fresh water. Yéil liked that water very much and drank it insatiably. He even thought about asking for some water to take with him, but was embarrassed to do so. After the meal, Yéil began telling Ganook about his own origin and also recounted the whole story of the creation of the world. Ganook listened for a while and finally began to doze off. Wishing to put him to sleep, Yéil kept talking, periodically saying, "Listen, *ax káani*, there is more to tell!" But no matter how entertaining Yéil's story was, Ganook could not overcome his drowsiness and finally was sound asleep, in his usual place, that is, on top of the well's lid. Then Yéil took some dog excrement and quietly placed it under Ganook. Having done the trick, he walked some distance away and began calling him, "*Ax káani*, get up! Look what you have done!"

Although sound asleep, Ganook woke up when he heard the news and, while turning over, dirtied his hand and immediately ran to the sea to wash. When this happened, Yéil rushed to open the lid and began to drink as much water as he could. When he had quenched his thirst and filled his mouth, Yéil immediately turned into a raven and flew into the smokehole of the house. Ganook, however, began yelling, "Stop him!" And so Yéil was stopped right in the opening, but who caused this is unknown. Ganook then built a fire and began smoking his guest as long as he wanted. This made Yéil black, while before that he was all white. Finally, Ganook took pity on him, got tired, and released Yéil who began flying toward his own land, dropping water from his mouth. Wherever those drops fell, lakes, rivers, springs and other receptacles of fresh water appeared.[77]

In the same manner Yéil obtained fire for mankind, which also had been missing from the earth. It could only be found in the middle of the sea, on some island. Yéil flew there and stole it. He found the island, took a smoldering firebrand in his strong beak and flew back as fast as he possibly could. That journey cost him half his beak. Along the way, the firebrand began to burn and Yéil was barely able to bring it ashore. As soon as he reached the shore, he threw it on the ground and the flying sparks hit rocks and trees. That is why today they contain fire and can be used to provide heat.

At first people could not obtain fire and heat from the forest, because the Master of the Forest prevented them. He caught and put a deadly sleep over any person who dared to enter the forest and steal firewood. Once again Yéil came to people's rescue. He went to the forest kingdom himself, found the people who had been put to sleep and woke them up miraculously. Here is how it happened. Thinking about the way to revive the sleeping people, found in the forest,[7] Yéil was walking along the seashore and saw a seagull swimming and nodding its head to him joyfully and complacently. "Why are you so happy, my friend, and what do you have?" asked Yéil. "I have the *sak*-fish [*saak*, candlefish, eulachen]," replied the seagull. "If it is true, show it to me," said Yéil. The seagull immediately flew from near the shore to the sea, dived in the water, caught the above mentioned fish, showed it to Yéil and ate it. Having left the seagull, Yéil continued walking and, upon meeting a heron, he said to it: "Do you know that the seagull is saying all sorts of bad things about you?" The heron became very angry, flew to the seagull immediately and attacked the innocent bird. As soon as it plunged its claws into the seagull's belly, the latter dropped the fish it had swallowed, which Yéil grabbed quickly.

Leaving the heron and the seagull fighting, he hurried on. After a while, he saw a *barabora* built on the seashore. Upon entering it, he saw a very old man whom he told, "You know, I have found *saak*." The man replied, "How is it possible, if I am the only one who has this fish and can give or send it . . . ." To convince the old man, Yéil showed him his fish and told him what he had seen and how he had obtained it. The old man became furious at the thief, but, realizing that it no longer made any sense to keep *saak* locked up, presented Yéil with a whole canoe filled with it. Yéil gratefully accepted that and departed from the old man in the canoe. As soon as the old man's territory was behind him, Yéil released all the fish into the sea. When people saw *saak* splashing on the beach, they all rushed to catch it in every possible way. In the meantime, Yéil was sitting in his canoe, enjoying the sight. Suddenly he noticed one woman who had also come to catch *saak* but was late. He said to her, "Would you like some fish? If you do, wade toward me."

The woman gladly began wading in his direction. When she was already in rather deep water and was forced to lift her clothes up to her shoulders, Yéil pulled several hairs from her armpit. Having rewarded her with *saak*, he hurried to the place where the dead people were lying in the forest. Using the woman's hairs, he began to tickle their nostrils, causing them to sneeze and come back to life. Thus he revived all the people killed by the Master of the Forest and then taught them how to obtain fire from wood.[8]

After that Yéil also taught people the art of shooting game with a bow and arrow and provided them with the game itself. At first people had no idea about the various types of fish, amphibious animals, such as hair seal [*nerpa*], fur seal [*morskoi kot*], otter [*vydra*], beaver [*bobr*], and game animals. The whole animal kingdom was controlled by a noble chief named Kanakhkatvaia [X'anaxgaat-waayáa].[78] X'anaxgaatwaayáa owned a large island, inaccessible to anybody except himself, where he guarded his treasure. Here is what the myth tells about Yéil procuring good arrows for the people and setting all the animals free.

When Yéil began his journey to the domain of X'anaxgaatwaayáa, he pondered the best way of dealing with this proud and suspicious owner who did not trust even his own daughter. Yéil was already approaching the boundary of X'anaxgaatwaayáa's land, but still had not decided what to do. Suddenly he met a hunter and got acquainted with him. The hunter turned out to be very talkative and spoke in detail about his own affairs, also mentioning a few things about X'anaxgaatwaayáa and his beautiful daughter. Yéil kept listening to his new acquaintance and asking questions but kept quiet about himself. He especially liked the hunter's arrows, which he would have loved to obtain but did not know how. In his usual manner, he decided to resort to deceit. He began praising the arrows and the hunter himself, who started to show off his skills even more. He took aim at small birds that were far away and killed them with the first shot. Yéil praised the hunter but, at the same time, let out the secret that he could shoot further with his own arrows. The hunter became interested and said, "Go ahead, try, and I'll watch."

And that was exactly what Yéil needed. Secretly he put a small blade of grass called *tliutl* [*lóol*, fireweed] on the tip of the arrow. This was not really grass but a bird, which can still be seen today, flying up and down—they call it a wagtail. The arrow was released and began to fly but was soon ready to fall in the wrong place. Then Yéil yelled, "raise it higher," and the arrow hit the target. The hunter was amazed by Yéil's dexterity and his ability to shoot that far. He offered to exchange arrows immediately and Yéil gave him his full consent.

As soon as the exchange had taken place, the two friends parted. Yéil went to the *taion*'s house. He knew that X'anaxgaatwaayáa had a beautiful daughter who had already been wooed by suitors. However, all of them had been rejected by X'anaxgaatwaayáa who did not like them. Yéil was hoping to please the old man with his arrows. After refusing to grant his permission for a long time, the old man finally agreed to the marriage. Yéil moved into the *taion*'s house and tried to be obedient, while observing and remembering everything.

The *taion* had a magical cane [*palka*], with an octopus tentacle carved on its end. By means of that cane X'anaxgaatwaayáa could pull up any object from any distance—such was its magical power. Finally Yéil got his hands on it. Once the old man began to trust Yéil completely, the latter started secretly testing the miraculous power of the cane. Things went quite well. Whatever creature Yéil pointed the cane at, e.g., a mountain goat or a whale playing in the distance, the latter would be immediately pulled toward him. However, he failed to pull up one little island in the middle of the bay where X'anaxgaatwaayáa kept his treasure and secrets. A castle[79] built on that island contained the most rare types of land and sea animals, but X'anaxgaatwaayáa would not allow anybody to go there, even Yéil. For a long time Yéil tried to get to that island but to no avail. He would frequently point the cane at the mysterious island but the island would not move toward him. Only once, when he pointed the cane while mentioning X'anaxgaatwaayáa's name, did he notice that the island seemed to be moving. Then Yéil began to sing:[80]

x'a-nax-gaat-waa-yáa
i a hee a a hiya a hee iya

x'a-nax̱-g̱aat-waa-yáa
ī a hee a a hiya a hee iya

The island began to move closer and closer, but as soon as it touched shore, [the castle] suddenly fell apart and all the animals in it—guinea pigs [?], hair seals [*nerpa*], beavers [*bobr*], etc.—ran away. Some began swimming in the sea, others scattered on land—whatever they chose became their habitat. Of course, after that act, Yéil had to run away from the *taion*.

Yéil lived on earth for a long time and acted as the benefactor of mankind. His adventures are countless. Sometimes rather funny things are told about him, for example, when he got inside a whale and built a fire there. This made the whale hot and forced it to climb ashore, where he remained forever as the people's catch.[81] Another funny story is told about Yéil hunting halibut in the company of the bear and the cormorant [*urila*].[82] Besides purely material comforts with which he rewarded people, Yéil also taught them various virtues. Thus he instructed that children should respect their parents and elders, that people should not wage war and shed blood, that they should not steal, lie, and should obey the rules of fasting and not pollute themselves, etc.[83] At the present time, Yéil rarely appears among the people. He now lives in the same place from where he had originally come: in the land of Nass, where the sun rises. There he has his celestial palaces [*chertogi*] that are very difficult to get to. Even [shaman's] spirits or *eki* [*yéik*] themselves are unable to do that. One teki-ek [apparently *dikée yéik*, spirit of the upper realm], tried to get there but was severely punished for his impertinence. His whole left side turned into stone because, while flying to the land of Nass, he did not look around and consequently one of his sides crushed into Yéil's palace.

Yéil still loves people and always tries to take care of them and help them. But he dislikes when they make fun of him and takes vengeance on the guilty persons, punishing them rather severely. Occasionally, in a fit of rage against the people, he sends them diseases and other misfortunes. His anger, however, is easy to mollify. All the orders from Yéil are brought to mankind by the eastern winds.

Yéil has a son whose mother is unknown. This son loves mankind even more than Yéil himself and often intercedes with his father on their behalf. He frequently carries out his father's orders, just as other gods do.[84]

CHAPTER VII

Other Deities of the Tlingit Indians: Khetl [Xeitl], Agishanuku [Haayeeshaanák'u], Tlianakhiduk [Tl'anaxéedákw], and Myths about Them.

Besides G̲anook and Yéil, Tlingit legends describe in detail the lives of two other deities, brother and sister—Xeitl and Haayeeshaanák'u. Their names are translated as follows: the first one means "thunderstorm," "echo," and the second one, "an old woman down below" or, "an old woman of the underworld." Nothing is known about their origin, except that when the great flood began, Xeitl, like Yéil, covered himself with the skin of a large bird and soared, travelling southeast, toward the celestial realms beyond the clouds, called *kutsgi* [*gus-s'yee*]*⁸⁵. There he settled permanently. When he was saying good-bye to his sister, who had to seek refuge on one of the high mountains, Xeitl told her that, although they might never see each other again, as long as he lived she would periodically hear from him.

Xeitl looks like a huge dragon-bird, with long thin wings, huge fiery eyes, and sharp claws. He spends most of his time on earth and rarely visits *kutsgi* [*gus'yee*] nowadays. Usually he sits quietly on the ridges of the northern mountains. Sometimes he flies down to the sea to hunt whales—his favorite food. Xeitl can easily grab one or two huge Pacific whales, lift them up into the air, and carry them to the bare, tall mountain tops where he eats them. This is as easy for him to do as for a seagull to catch a small fish. The Tlingit, who often find deposits of bones of huge antediluvian animals, and whole skeletons of mastodons and other monsters, in the ledges of high mountains, are fully convinced that these are the remains of Xeitl's meal.*⁸⁶

Whenever Xeitl awakens from his inactivity and begins stretching out his wings, the air around him starts to move so swiftly that a real storm begins. Thus, a storm with thunder and lightning, and cyclones on land and at sea are nothing else but the terrible flight of Xeitl. Thunder is the noise made by his wings, lightning—the shine of his eyes, and whirlwinds and cyclones—the result of the flapping of his wings. Just as Xeitl seizes whales with his powerful claws, he occasionally pulls huge trees out of the ground, turns ships over, destroys buildings, and burns everything with the shine and flame of his eyes.

Once a year, or sometimes more often, Xeitl visits the Island of Edgecumbe [Kruzof Island], located near the Island of Sitka [Baranof Island], and other nearby places. The reason for these visits is his sister's descent underground from the top of Mt. Edgecumbe. To escape the flood, Haayeeshaanák'u climbed to the very top of this mountain, but the water covered even the top itself and forced her to disappear inside the earth. One could still see a huge crater at the place where the earth had received her. Haaɣeeshaanák'u still lives underneath this mountain which stands right in the middle of the earth. Xeitl flies to Mt. Edgecumbe to let his sister know that he is still alive.

Although Haaɣeeshaanák'u lives underground, she loves mankind. It is only thanks to her that the earth and the people still exist. In a fit of rage against mankind, Xeitl has tried a number of times to destroy the earth. Many times he came close to the pole supporting the earth and tried to pull it from its proper place. He would have succeeded if not for Haaɣeeshaanák'u's resistance. She tried to induce Xeitl not to destroy the earth and its people, and sometimes simply used force to pull or push him away from the pole.[*87] The people learn about this struggle from earthquakes and underground rumble. Haaɣeeshaanák'u is not very comfortable in her underground home. Sometimes it is quite cold down there and the poor old woman must constantly keep a fire burning to stay warm. The smoke from the fire can be seen from the top of Mt. Edgecumbe.[9] In order to please and help Haaɣeeshaanák'u, the Tlingit build fires on the ground thinking that this method warms the earth, and thus makes Haaɣeeshaanák'u happy. To prevent the earth from cracking, when Xeitl shakes the pole supporting it, the Indians, upon hearing the rumble, come out of their house and sit down on the ground to engage in a tug-of-war. They believe that this helps Haaɣeeshaanák'u to overpower Xeitl. They even have special songs composed for this occasion, which the crowd sings during earthquakes, accompanied by the tapping of gambling sticks [igral'nye kostiashki i palochki], while young men play a tug-of-war.[*88]

There is another, even greater benefactor of the Tlingit Indians—a female goddess named Tl'anaxéedákw. Even today the Tlingit still believe in this miraculous woman, a simple encounter with whom brings great luck. She lives on earth and appears to people in some isolated places, such as the bank of a large river or a lake. Sometimes she can be seen simultaneously by several people. One usually sees her naked, bathing in the water or walking along the shore, lulling a child she carries in her arms. At first one hears only the splashing of water or the sound of her lulling (resembling the buzzing of a wild bee), and then notices Tl'anaxéedákw herself. Nobody, however, has taken a good look at her face yet. She is believed to be beautiful. She has gorgeous dark green hair reaching almost to her feet and covering her slender body.

The myth about this goddess tells that she had once been a water spirit or a mermaid. Living in a large lake with her girl friends, mermaids like her, Tl'anaxéedákw knew no troubles or sorrows. None of her girl friends was as fond of making fun of people as she. When a hunter pursuing his prey would accidentally wander into the vicinity of the lake, Tl'anaxéedákw was the first one to start playing tricks on him. She would splash and click in the thick reeds like a beaver, snort like a bear catching fish, or imitate the voices of several animals and birds. In this manner she would lead the hunter all around the lake, until

68

he lost all his strength, fell into the water and drowned. She found great pleasure in this tormenting and killing of hunters. Even her friends, the mermaids, found this behavior cruel. For a long time she got away with all those tricks. Many human beings were lured by her to the bottom of the deep lake. But fate finally punished her, and here is how it happened.

A young hunter began visiting the shores of the lake. He was so skilled in the use of the bow and arrow, that he easily killed all sorts of game. Within an hour he would kill a sufficient quantity of various valuable animals and birds, and then would come close to the lake and sit there, deep in his thoughts, until darkness covered the earth. Then, still preoccupied, he would reluctantly return to his native village. In the same mood, he would come back to the lake the next morning. He was always alone, without friends or relatives. Sadness never disappeared from his handsome face. The playful mermaid noticed the new visitor and did not miss the opportunity to make him the object of her tricks. At first she began making fun of him, but to her surprise and anger, the young man paid no attention whatsoever to her and her jokes. As before, having killed enough game, he would sit at the shore, in the shadow of old cedar trees, absorbed in his deep secret thoughts. No matter what took place around him, the hunter seemed not to see or hear anything. When night came, he left, with the same sad expression on his face, and went to a place between two high mountain peaks covered with evergreen cedars and snow caps. There, on the sea shore, fires were burning, and around them the hunter's kinsmen, the great tribe of *Tlianiety* [*Laa*ɣ*aneidi'* or *Laa*ɣ*ineidi*], joyfully and loudly passed their monotonous life day by day.

This went on almost the entire summer. The mermaid became so used to seeing the hunter, that she felt lonely when he did not appear for some reason. After such intervals, his arrival made her happy. Looking at his handsome, sad face, she began feeling sorry for him. Little by little her jokes stopped. When autumn came and then winter, the surface of the lake became covered with a thick layer of ice, so that one could no longer swim and splash, and see the hunter, and the mermaid became sad. Impatiently she waited for the arrival of spring. It was still cold. The bears had not come down from the high mountains for their regular hunting and deep mountain valleys were still snow-covered, when the hunter returned to the shores of the lake. Its surface was not yet completely clear of ice. But the mermaid was already appearing on the surface and was getting happier every day. Her joyful days had come back.

Finally, the hunter abided at the lake in the company of the mermaid not only during the day but at night as well. Throughout the summer, he almost never appeared in his native village where his tribesmen lived. The inhabitants of the lake began to worry about their girl friend's behavior. And they did have a reason to worry. Soon it was no longer a secret to anyone that the mermaid had been made pregnant by an ordinary mortal. And so all the inhabitants of the lake turned away from her. At the same time, her lover, having learned of her condition, began to lose interest in the former object of his passion. Once he was even unfaithful to her. This the mermaid could not tolerate at all and, as the story goes, she scratched the unfaithful one rather badly. The latter, in turn, pierced the jealous but passionately loving heart of the mermaid with his knife.

Since then, the spirit of the mermaid wanders on earth with her baby. The mermaids expelled Tl'anaxéedákw from their company, but she cannot join the company of human beings either. Thus the poor one wanders between the two, but always stays closer to human beings. She feels guilty toward them, for having destroyed so many innocent people just for fun. Therefore, with every good opportunity, she acts as their benefactor, trying to make up for old wrongs.[89]

Tl'anaxéedákw is always seen before a great fortune or luck . . . . Thus the Tlingit saw her in Yakutat, not long before their first destruction of a Russian colony in 1805, when they unexpectedly attacked the Russian settlers on July 29 and slaughtered all of them. She was also seen near the village of Auk, at the exact spot where later on gold was discovered and where the town of Juneau is now located. At the present time, when most Tlingit Indians, with very few exceptions, are Christians, the pagan goddess Tl'anaxéedákw is often confused with the Mother of God.[90]

Generally speaking, as it frequently happens during a shift from pagan religion to Christianity, the Tlingit quite often transfer their pagan ideas to Christianity. Just as the Russian Slavs transferred attributes of the pagan god Volos to St. Vlasii and the Saints Flor and Lavr, and as certain characteristics of Perun were acquired by the prophet Elijah, etc., so, among the Tlingit, Xeitl's qualities are now partially transferred to the prophet Elijah, Ganook is confused with Noah, and so on. The time is near when these legends will become simply amusing tales. They already no longer influence everyday life. Even if somebody still believes in the existence of Yéil, Ganook and other countless gods and goddesses, this belief is not expressed in any definite cult, and hence, remains inactive.[91] However, Tlingit beliefs in the afterlife, the transmigration of the souls and spirits, in general, is a different story altogether. This type of faith is still deeply rooted in the soul of the Indians. It is frequently their inner, most cherished faith, untouched by Christian evangelization, which in its subsequent development served as the basis of shamanism.

CHAPTER VIII

Beliefs in Spirits and Souls of the Dead.

The Indian has populated the entire world with spirits or *yéik*. A *yéik* is a spiritual being capable of influencing man indirectly, by assuming the guise of a live creature (a human being, an animal, a fish, etc.), or directly, as an invisible force, in most cases, an evil, harmful one. A *yéik* can even inhabit material objects, for example, trees, rocks, grass, idols [carved figures], etc. *Yéik* are distinguished according to their place of residence or habitat. In the opinion of the Tlingit, some *yéik* dwell up above, in the sky. Therefore they are called *tekieki* [apparently *dikée yéigi*] or spirits of the above. Other *yéik* live down below, in the water, underground, or in caves, and are hence called *tygieki* [apparently *diyée yéigi*] or spirits of the below. The third category of *yéik* live on earth but somewhere far away, at its edge. For some reason they are called *takiyeigi* [*daagi yéigi ?*] and their dwelling place is called *takanku* [*dagankú*].[*92]

Nothing definite is known about the origin of the *yéik*. Equally unknown is whether their life has some sort of end or whether, as noncorporeal spirits, they live forever. In Tlingit myths, where *yéik* play a significant role, they are confused and often fully identified with the souls of the dead. The latter are said to inhabit the same domain as the *yéik*: some live above, some live below, and some—far away, in the north. All of the human souls are called by the general name *kaeki* [*kaa yéigi*], from the word *ka* [*káa*],[*93] "human being," and *yéik*, "spirit." Because of this, one has to study the ideas about *yéik* and *kaa yéigi* together.

The Tlingit believe that a person's death is only the beginning of a new life, often better than the one he has led before. Having a strong faith in the existence of a spiritual world, life after death, and constant interaction between the visible material and the spiritual worlds, the Tlingit Indian is not afraid of dying and does not view death as something unusual and terrifying. In his imagination, the world beyond the grave and the corporeal one are so closely linked to each other, that the transition between them seems to be very simple and natural. The most pleasant death is believed to be that of a warrior killed on the battle field. The souls of such people go directly to the dwelling place of the *dikée yéigi*, or to what is called *kiuakau* [*keewakáawu*].[*94] Here they are waited on by [the souls of] the enemies they have slain, as well as the slaves or *kalgi* [sing. *kalga*] strangled during the mortuary feast given in their honor.

Somewhat worse off are the souls of those who after death join the company of the *daagi yéigi* in *dagankú*. But the worst fate awaits the souls joining the *diyée yéigi* in the place called *tsikekau* [*s'igeekáawu*], where Tagi-ankau [Diyée

71

Aankáawu, lit. "chief of the below"] or Satan himself dwells. The Indian *s'igeekáawu* or hell, however, was not as terrifying a place as Dante's Hell, and the Diyée Aankáawu was not a very evil spirit."[95]

The difference between *s'igeekáwu*, *keewakáawu*, and *dagankú* is the following. In *keewakáawu* the souls live prosperously, with plenty of warmth, light, and food, especially grease. They live rather comfortably in *dagankú* as well, but it is difficult to get there. The road there is not easy, especially when the relatives of the deceased cry a lot. This forces the soul to walk to *dagankú* over water and tundra. However, the difficulty of this journey and some of the inconveniences of life in *dagankú* can be eased. To do this, relatives of the deceased have to give memorial feasts in his honor and make offerings [to him] by throwing pieces of food into the fire. To prevent the soul from getting cold during the journey and while living in *dagankú* itself, the body of the deceased should always be cremated, especially when it comes to ordinary people whose souls have no chance of entering *keewakáawu*. If bodies of such people are not cremated, their souls are miserable in the afterworld. They have no right to approach the common fire, where the souls of the dead whose bodies have been cremated warm themselves. They have to shiver from cold forever and enviously watch from a distance the lucky ones sitting by the warm fire. As far as the poor souls in *s'igeekáawu* are concerned, they too suffer from hunger and cold.[10]

The Tlingit Indian strongly believes in the transmigration of the souls of the dead, assuming that the soul can come back to earth after being reborn in another human or animal form."[96] He believes that a deceased member of the family can be reborn through one of the women of the same group. This fact is easy to establish: the deceased would begin to appear to the pregnant woman in her dreams or she would occasionally hear his voice in the waking life. In such cases, the newly born is given the name of the deceased.

There are also cases of souls being reborn through animals—bear, hair seal, dog, deer, etc. There are many reasons for the soul of one person to be reborn in human form and that of another—in animal form, but these are difficult to understand. First of all, every person has his own *yéik*, always taking care of him and protecting him from dangers in difficult circumstances of life. This *yéik* is called *tukinaek* [*du kinaayéigi*, "his spirit above"] and is a kind and friendly spirit, always directing man to goodness and turning him away from evil."[97] In some cases, however, it can abandon man altogether. Man's destiny after death depends on *du kinaayéigi*. The latter determines whether the soul is sent to *keewakáawu* or *s'igeekáawu*, which, in turn, determines the subsequent fate of the soul. From *keewakáawu* and *dagankú*, the souls of the dead usually return in human form and, depending on circumstances, their own inclinations, and the merits of their former lives, become once again brave warriors or slaves. Sometimes things change and a poor slave, having spent his entire life in misery and poverty, is reincarnated into the body of a warrior and can even become a military leader. From *s'igeekáawu*, however, the souls of the dead have to transmigrate into animals. Tlingit mythology does not provide a definite answer to the question of which particular sins determine the transmigration into a particular animal. In ancient times, the Tlingit mythology, like that of the Egyptians, probably had a definite code of such sins and differentiated grave sins from less significant ones, but this differentiation lost its original form after their religion degenerated into crude shamanism.

A definite evidence of the existence in ancient time of the belief in the possibility of transmigration of the human soul into a land otter *(kushta [kóoshdaa])*, brown bear *(xóots)*, sea otter, petrel, etc., is the surviving notion that these animals have human souls and can understand human speech. This explains why in the past the Indians never killed these animals and even today avoid killing them without a special reason. In former times, to kill them was considered a great shame.

The Indians have many stories about the land otter and the bear, indicating their close spiritual affinity with man, as well as their ability to understand him. They say that a land otter pursued by a hunter would sometimes stop and speak with a human voice, asking for mercy. Its meat is never eaten, but buried in the ground after the skin has been removed. Such attitudes toward the land otter are the result of some resemblances between this animal and man, not only in some of its habits but in the structure of its body.

The bear is respected even more. When an Indian goes into the forest for something and is afraid of meeting a bear, he tries to prevent this and to appease the animal with various praises and kind nicknames. Otherwise, if one begins scolding the bear and laughing at its weaknesses and imperfections, one could anger it and bring trouble upon oneself, because the animal not only understands what people say but can scent approaching enemies or unfriendly people from a great distance. In addition, the bear possesses the same capabilities of understanding and feeling as man does. He is characterized by honesty, pride, generosity, vengeance, and other human qualities. He can even feel shame characteristic of the different sexes. Thus there is a belief that a [male] bear would run away when confronted with human female nakedness.

Bear hunting, among the Tlingit, is accompanied by numerous omens, spells, and rituals, strongly resembling those of the northern Eskimos, Greenland Eskimos, and our own Siberian natives. Greenland Eskimo women, upon noticing a bear nearby, expose the upper part of their body in order to chase him away. And when a bear is killed, but before it is butchered, Greenland Eskimos take turns to come up to it, drink its warm blood, and then slap the soft fur with their hand while repeating "you are fat, you are very fat." When a bear's head is cut off, it is taken inside the *barabora*, placed upon a table and decorated with various trinkets. The bear's ears and nostrils are plugged up, which according to these savages, should prevent all bears that they hunt from smelling the approaching human beings. The head of the bear is kept in this condition for five days and is not eaten, because of the fear that the bear's soul would die on its way home. Eskimos believe that the bear's soul never returns home before the fifth day . . . . [98]

Just like these Greenlanders, the Alaskan Indians, after killing a bear, drink its blood and eat its heart before they lose their warmth. They are convinced that by doing it they are honoring the entire bear race and that it would make them brave and strong as a bear. The head of the slain bear is decorated with feathers and placed near the fire, where the Indians sing songs in its honor, so as to have success in future bear hunts. At that time, all immodest words and especially sneers, have to be strictly avoided, because they are considered sinful. The bear race would have avenged any desecration or insult, even those committed against one of their slain relatives. The soul of a bear remains alive after its death and can inform its relatives about the insults . . . . For the same reason, women going into the woods to pick berries or gather roots sing songs in honor of the bear and, upon seeing its tracks, begin praising him, fearing that otherwise they would be taken to its den. When accidentally stumbling upon a bear, Tlingit women, like the Greenland Eskimo, uncover the upper part of their body, convinced that the bear would be embarrassed and would run away.

By the way, here is a story, told about one girl, a *taion*'s daughter, who made fun of the bear. On one autumn day, a *taion*'s daughter went berry-picking into the woods, in the company of her girl friends. While crossing a bear's path along the way, she began scolding the bear, calling it stupid, blind, clumsy, etc. Several times her friends tried to persuade her to stop, but she would not listen and continued making fun of the bear. When it was time to go back home with the berries, those of the *taion*'s daughter fell out of her basket and scattered on the ground. This happened three times. At first, her friends helped her gather the scattered berries, but then decided to leave her alone, seeing that it was getting dark and thinking that there must have been some special reason why her berries would keep falling out like that.

A dark night set in. The poor girl had completely lost her way. Not knowing where to go, she sat down under a tree and fell asleep. Suddenly, in the middle of the night, she heard the familiar voice of her beloved, woke up and saw him in the darkness. She was so happy that she did not even know what to do. The man ordered her to follow him. She walked holding his hand for a long time, but instead of reaching a path or the edge of the forest, they were going further into the depths of the woods. The forest kept getting denser and denser. Finally, she could not stand it any longer and asked her companion how soon they would reach home. "Here it is, our home," he answered, "climb in there." In front of them was a large entrance into a bear den. The girl became frightened and stood in bewilderment. But her companion insisted and forced her to get inside. As soon as she descended inside the den, she stumbled upon two huge old bears and recoiled in fear. She tried to run away but her companion stopped her, saying that the two were human beings and only appeared to be bears to her. The girl climbed back into the den and did see an old couple standing in front of her. They looked very respectable and began inviting her kindly to come in further and not to be shy. Her companion followed her. But as soon as he entered, he suddenly turned from a man into an animal. He began reprimanding and reproaching her for scolding and laughing at him. Then he explained to her that bears inside their den are like ordinary human beings, and only outside of it have an animal appearance. At first the girl was upset but, after some time spent in the den, she fell in love with the young bear, became his wife, and even began to look like a bear.

She lived like that until the spring, when hunters found the den and killed the bears, first the old ones and then the young one. They wanted to kill the *taion*'s daughter as well, but having recognized the hunters as her brothers, she yelled with a human voice, telling them to spare her life because she was their missing sister. The whole story ended with her returning home and telling how bears live.[*99]

There are several concrete expressions of the belief in the similarity between the spiritual nature of men and animals, e.g., shamanistic incantations said over a patient or during divinations and on other occasions; animal masks inhabited, according to Tlingit belief, by spirits or *yéik* of animals. During these incantations, the shaman wishing to have a particular spirit serve him, e.g., that of a bear, puts on a mask representing that particular animal. The supernatural power of the *yéik* of animals and of human beings is almost the same. However, judging by the fact that, during a ceremony, animal *yéik* are invoked more often that those of human beings or of ancestors and famous people, animal *yéik* seem to be considered stronger and more powerful. The existence of an Indian belief in the possibility of the transmigration of human souls into animals is supported by the fact that most Tlingit names are those of animals.[*100] By giving his child an animal name, the Indian believes that it provides his descendant with the power and skills of the particular animal whose name he would carry.

CHAPTER IX

Belief in Afterlife. Funeral Rites. Attitudes Toward the Remains of the Dead.

The funeral rites as well as the feasts and celebrations in honor of the dead serve as an illustration of how clearly and vividly the Tlingit conceive of the soul's existence after death. Death of a family or clan member is deeply mourned by the relatives. When they notice the signs of the imminent demise of a sick person, they begin washing and dressing him in his best clothes, while he is still alive.[101] Several expensive blankets are wrapped around him and a *nakhen* [*naax- ein*, Chilkat blanket] is placed on top. Laid out around the deathbed of the deceased are his weapons and armor, his clan heirlooms, such as hats, masks, *sheshukhi* [plural of *sheishóox*, rattle], staffs and so forth, as well as other clan regalia which the deceased used while being the head of a *barabora* or a whole clan. All those objects used by the deceased in daily life, in hunting and other subsistence activities, such as knives, a pipe, tobacco, etc., were often wrapped in blankets and placed with the corpse. All these things were supposed to be useful for the deceased in the other world.

The mournful mood of the relatives is expressed by a strict fast which all the women of the *barabora*, and especially the wife and daughters of the deceased, impose upon themselves.[102] During the entire period while the deceased lies in the *barabora*, they sit around his body without moving; here they also sleep at night and cry from time to time. In addition to these mourners a few are also hired from the outside [of the matrilineal kin of the deceased]. The male relatives also express sorrow but in their own way. During this time they abstain from work. All of the various tasks involved in the funeral are performed by the wife's relatives, the people of the other blood and tribe [moiety].

While the corpse lies in the *barabora*, memorial feasts [*piry-pominki*] are held daily. During them guests receive food and in addition such gifts as blankets and whole pieces of linen and of other fabrics. Guests always leave loaded with food of various kinds. The deceased lies in the *barabora* for three days and sometimes longer. In the meantime, a pyre is prepared behind the *barabora* for the crema- tion of the corpse. The rectangular pyre made of dry spruce logs five to six feet long is filled with dry chips and brushwood, and then various greases are poured over it.

When everything is ready, the body of the deceased is carried outside, which is accompanied by some rituals. In ancient times, *kalgi* or slaves were killed at the moment, and their bodies were later cremated with the corpse of their master; it was hoped that the latter would not remain without slaves in the other world. The corpse itself was taken out not through the door but through the smokehole.[103] After the corpse, a live dog was also thrown from the fireplace into the opening. It is difficult to tell the meaning of these rites. Probably it is the same as that of early human sacrifices, i.e., the ashes were thrown after the deceased so that he would not suffer from cold in the other world. The dog, without which the Indian cannot survive on earth for a single day, could also become useful in the other world.[104] While the procession with the corpse, accompanied by female mourners, with their hair loose and faces painted, was moving toward the pyre, in the *barabora*, gifts were being distributed in memory of the deceased for the last time. The deceased was not laid but seated upon the pyre. Wrapped in blankets, with his face painted [with symbols of his clan] and his head covered with a black kerchief or a fur hat used by shamans, he resembled a live person from a distance. Artifacts destined for cremation with the body were arranged around it. Family crests—if one could use this term to refer to tribal emblems or totems—were usually not burned but passed on to the heir.

While the four or five persons in charge of cremation [*mogil'shchiki*] arranged the corpse, a whole choir of funeral singers gathered around the pyre. As a tambourine began to sound, the singers struck up a mournful song, tapping their bone rattles and sticks in time with it. The pyre was lit from different sides. The female mourners performed their last task with their backs to the pyre. To make the corpse burn up faster the men in charge of cremation turned it from side to side with long poles, until together with the pyre it turned into ashes and coals. The remains were collected and sometimes buried in the ground[105] or put in a box which was then placed inside a small house-monument [grave house] called *kakhety* [*ḵaa daakeidí*]. This is how the pagan Indians buried all their dead, rich or poor, with the exception of shamans.[106]

Shamans' corpses were never cremated. The Tlingit are convinced that their bodies do not decay, and therefore they are neither burned nor buried in the ground. When a shaman dies his relatives dress him in his special costume and keep him inside the *barabora* for four days, carrying the body from one corner of the house to another every day. Why this is done nobody knows. On the fifth day the corpse wrapped in blankets and tied to a board is taken to a secluded island where nobody can disturb it and left in a grave house, which is sometimes raised on small posts. The box with the shaman's charms [*talismany*] is left here as well. The shaman's corpse is usually left in a sitting posture. In the vicinity of Sitka there were quite a few such coffins with shamans' corpses. The Indians themselves are afraid to approach them. Even if they have to pass by an island where such grave houses are located, they make offerings in memory of the shaman lying there. They throw a few pinches of tobacco or grease into the sea, or, having come very close to the island, leave some food on the shore. They believe that the spirit of the shaman likes that.

However, idle American tourists gladly steal these corpses to place them in museums. Not too long ago three shamans' graves used to be pointed out near

Sitka. Incidentally, one of them was located in a cave or rather in a cleft of a cliff. Here the corpse of a gigantic shaman resting against the wall in a sitting posture remained untouched for several decades. But recently it disappeared. Many shamans, however, were buried in the ground by the Indians themselves who began to notice traces of the unwanted visitors. The latter always carried off something as a souvenir; sometimes a tuft of a shaman's hair, sometimes a decoration of the face—a nosepin, an earring, and so forth.

The Indians are greatly surprised that the white people treat the remains of the dead so disrespectfully; but what amazes them even more is the fact that the whites get away with such sacrilegious acts. The Indians themselves firmly believe that every grave house of a shaman is inhabited by one of his *yéik* who guards the peace of the deceased. The shaman, of course, has to be a real one, who observes rules of abstinence. Even the wildest nature stands in awe of him. For example, when ancient trees shading the remains of a shaman grow old and are no longer able to stand up, they never allow themselves to fall upon his grave house but fall elsewhere, not far from it. Similarly, when the posts supporting the *kaa daakeidí* become rotten, they do not collapse one at a time but all together, so as not to disturb the position of the shaman's corpse.

Half a year or so after the funeral of an ordinary Indian or a shaman, their relatives organize big festivities in memory of the deceased. However, these festivities do not differ much from ordinary feasts given by the Tlingit on various occasions.

CHAPTER X

Shamanism and Its Asiatic Origin. Ikht [Ĩxt'] and Nukstsaty [Nakws'aatĩ]. Shamanistic Rituals. Curing of the Sick Afflicted by Witchcraft.

The common origin of the peoples inhabiting all parts of the world is being confirmed daily with increasingly stronger evidence. Just recently American newspapers announced a discovery made by one Russian linguist who had found irrefutable evidence of the similarity between the language of the Asiatic natives inhabiting the northeastern coast of Siberia and American Indian languages. In an article published in the January- February 1903 [1902] issue of *The American Antiquarian*, Mr. Charles Hallock attempts to solve the problem of the origin of the American Indians on the basis of archaeological discoveries made in Mexico and other parts of the American continent.[107] He concludes that the ancient ancestors of the Mexican Indians were colonists from Korea, which at the time was under Chinese domination. In his opinion, this event occurred in the first half of the sixth century A.D. and is confirmed by Chinese manuscripts as well as similarities in languages, customs, and proficiency in the arts and architecture. He thinks that their writing system was exclusively hieroglyphic and that this medium of communication was spread across the whole continent. "History shows," says he, "that the Koreans migrated to escape tyranny, undertaking a sea voyage of nine weeks to the northeast. No matter who first peopled Central America, the Koreans certainly were in communication with America as far back as the second year of the dynasty of Tsin, Emperor of China, who declared war against Korea" and so on. There is, however, even stronger evidence of the Asiatic origin of the Indians, at least the Alaskan Indians, than these conjectures of Mr. Hallock and other scholars. This evidence is the religious beliefs, and especially the shamanistic cult, that once existed among the Alaskan Indians and is still adhered to by some of them.

The resemblance between this form of shamanism and that of the northeastern inhabitants of Siberia is striking, especially as far as shamanistic decorations and paraphernalia used in performances are concerned. According to the descriptions of the content of those famous one hundred and thirty-six boxes, which have just arrived in Washington from Siberia for the American Museum of Natural History, this resemblance very often becomes an almost total identity. Musical instruments, face masks, stone and clay artifacts are absolutely identical to those found before and those still existing in Alaska. Combined with other descriptions made by the so-called Gessup [Jesup North Pacific] Expedition, all this resolves the question of the constant interaction between the inhabitants of Asia and America, existing since most ancient times. Therefore the description of the Alaskan shamanism is also interesting from a missionary point of view, at least for those who are concerned with the religious destiny of Siberia. On the other hand, if one keeps in mind that the Alaskan shamanism is, in essence, the same as that of all other American natives, its discussion acquires a scientific interest as well.[*108]

In order to understand and evaluate the significance and influence of shamanism on the life of savages, the reader has to take into account those special circumstances and conditions (poorly known to the civilized man) of the past and even the present life of the Alaskan natives. Obviously one cannot deny the powerful influence of nature on man. It is not easy for a wild man to penetrate the mysteries of God's Wisdom [*premudrost'*]. The formidable forces of nature make him tremble with fear, before any reflection can begin. If these forces help him, the fear is mixed with gratitude and adoration. This is particularly true of such natural elements as water, fire and air, which he encounters daily, either fighting them or using their help and benefiting from them. In his imagination, those crude religious ideas to which he adheres become even cruder, sometimes resembling Australian fetishism.

Severe climate, the mountain tops always snow covered, the stormy northern sea surrounding the peninsula and the islands, the impenetrable forests evergreen but unfriendly—all of this inspires deep fear in the northern man, whose natural spiritual endowments are rather poor. The harsh North yields nothing without a struggle. But even in his fight against the northern nature, man does not achieve much, except for the things necessary to drag out a miserable existence of a semihuman-semianimal creature. This is why, perhaps, we do not find in Alaska remains of big cities, temples and other gigantic structures that have made Central American and areas of ancient Asian civilizations so famous. The North did not allow culture to develop; on the contrary, it gradually froze out those traces of culture that the ancestors of the Alaskan inhabitants had brought from their ancient birthplace. Therefore, it is not surprising that the shamanistic cult of the Tlingit Indians contains wild rituals and primitive notions similar to fetishism, while their belief in witches and witchcraft is stronger than anywhere else.

Strictly speaking, Tlingit shamanism consists of two types of belief—belief in the shaman or íxt' and in the witch or nakws'aatí. One should never confuse the two, although, as we shall see below, their character and activity have much in common. Indians believe that the only way to become a shaman is to be born with a special talent for it. If nature endows a person with such a talent, it can be detected in very early childhood. While still a child, a future shaman avoids human company, seeks solitude, talks to himself, and even his appearance is different from that of other children. From early childhood, his hair is twisted into little braids like those worn by adult shamans. Unlike other children, he dislikes comfort. From his early days, he eats the most coarse food and is not afraid of heat or cold. But the most definite sign that the child will grow up to be a shaman is the occasional visits of *yéik* or spirits.

Nevertheless, not every child with predisposition to shamanism can grow up to be a shaman. This requires not only a desire but certain efforts on the part of the person chosen by nature for this task. To be a shaman means to have at one's disposal a certain number of *yéik* or spirits who would be brought to him by means of certain rituals and incantations, and would obediently carry out all his orders. For example, they would reveal any mysteries, including those of the future, and especially those concerning evil people—first and foremost, the *nakws'aatí* or witches; they would also aid those whom the shaman wishes to help, etc.

To acquire *yéik*, the person aspiring to become a shaman has to go into seclusion and observe an exhausting fast. Usually the candidate goes to a small isolated island, one of those that are so numerous in southern Alaska, where the coast is dotted with curiously shaped bays and straits. This journey is kept secret from everybody, except maybe his closest kin. Here, face to face with the wild, mysterious, and formidable nature, he begins his exploits. Century-old spruce trees and cedars that prevent sunlight from penetrating the forest serve as his cover. When everything is quiet, and only the sound of the surf lightly touching the rocky shore can be heard, these ancient giants slowly sink into a lazy slumber. Only somewhere up above, their majestic crowns whisper lightly, rustling their branches. But how terrifying is their cracking noise when the gusty wind starts hitting their heads. This mysterious and frightening noise, along with the rumble and roar of the ocean waves crashing against the rocks, makes every living creature tremble. Animals and birds hide in their shelters. A shy deer seeks refuge among the rocks, under the cover of high cliffs. Every creature is terrified, but the future shaman does not share this feeling. He listens carefully to the howling of the storm and the noise of the forest and the sea, as to voices from that mysterious world that he intends to apprehend. This is the voice of the elements that he wants to learn to dominate and command. The fast and all kinds of other abstentions are the means of coming closer to this mysterious world, poorly understood by ordinary people.

For several days or even months, the shaman has to eat only the bark of the devilclub [*nezamainik, Oploponax horridus*]—a shrub whose leaves and stems are covered with large thorns. The shaman can drink only salt water. This fast lasts until gradually *yéik* begin to appear and the shaman himself reaches a state when he is able to enter a trance and call those *yéik* that are needed. This means that he has reached the first stage in his development as a shaman. There is now definite hope that the spiritual and material forces of nature will obey him. But he cannot practice yet, because that requires having other tools of shamanism. They are the tongue of a land otter, various masks, a *sheishóox* or rattle used by the shaman to call his spirits, a hat trimmed with marten fur (*s'áaxw*), a staff or magic wand *(íxt' wootsaagáɣi)*, and so forth.

The most difficult task is to obtain a land otter's tongue. Prior to the coming of white people to Alaska, when the Tlingit were afraid of committing the sin of killing their fellow man in the guise of a land otter, there were plenty of these animals everywhere, and one could encounter them on any island. Hence a candidate for shamanism could easily meet a land otter, but was not allowed to kill it with any weapon. He could not even use a stone or stick but had to rely on the power of his word. He had to come close to the land otter and kill it by uttering the sound "o" in various tones. A powerful shaman made the land otter fall flat on its back, with its tongue sticking out, and die after the first utterance. The tongue was what the shaman was after. He cut it out, while uttering various sacred formulae, and had to keep it for the rest of his life, carrying it on his chest. Other shamanistic paraphernalia were easier to obtain. The best of them were those previously used by one or several shamans. It was assumed that along with the artifacts the heir acquired the magical power of their previous owner. Ancient *sheishóox* or rattles were considered particularly valuable.

Every shaman had a small box or chest where he kept all of his paraphernalia mentioned above as well as other magical objects: bone knives, strips of hide for tying around the shaman's body during seances, pieces of clothing belonging to a famous deceased shaman, locks of his hair, his fingernail, a bone from his finger or toe, his tooth, etc. The shaman could never cut his own hair. To prevent it from bothering him, the hair was pasted together with sticky spruce sap. Having turned into large and long matted braids and locks, the hair accompanied every shaman's movement, with its crackling sound resembling the one made by wooden balls when they hit one another. The most abstinent shaman did not engage in sexual relations at all, although celibacy was not required. Simple abstinence and fasting were required, however, especially when the shaman was carrying out his duties. Tlingit believed that this abstinence determined the degree of a shaman's power. *Yéik* do not obey a shaman that is not abstinent, but are fond of the one that is, and come to him even without being called. Tlingit stories about shamans are the best illustrations of how great their magical power can be. The following story is told about one Sitka shaman who lived in the 1840s.[*109]

One day he ordered his relatives and assistants to take him in a canoe to a bay near the Chistye Islands [?] (behind Mt. Edgecumbe) and throw him overboard. When they brought him to the designated bay, he ordered them to stop in its exact center, tie him up and wrap him in matting, and lower him to the bottom of the sea. His tenderhearted relatives did not know that the whole affair would end in an extraordinary miracle and thus refused for a long time to carry out their shaman's requests. But he kept insisting and they had to obey, no matter how much they pitied him. And so they tied a strap made of an enchanted land otter's skin to the shaman wrapped in matting, lifted him up and, having uttered a special sound four times, lowered him into the sea. The shaman went down faster than a stone or a slain whale, so that they barely had enough time to pay out the strap. Gradually the shaman stopped and his assistants tied an inflated bladder of the same land otter to the end of the strap. They remained at that spot for a while but noticed nothing unusual and went back to shore to mourn their famous kinsman. Next morning they returned to examine the place where the shaman had been thrown overboard but found nothing remarkable, except for the bladder still floating in the water. The same thing was observed on the third day. On the fourth day they returned again but found nothing and finally, having talked things over, decided to go back home to mourn the poor old man. All of a sudden they heard a sound of the drums used during shamanistic performances. The astonished relatives of the shaman followed that sound and came to one absolutely plumb cliff. There they saw a multitude of birds (the kind that exist only in Sitka), and on the side of the cliff was their shaman, lying prostrate with his head down, but unharmed. Blood was pouring out of his mouth, flowing over his face, but the shaman was alive and singing songs. His kinsmen used every effort to reach up to him and finally took him off the cliff. When they laid him down in the canoe, he was lying as if nothing had happened; soon he recovered, became bright and cheerful, and ordered them to sail home.

Another shaman is said to have managed to keep smallpox, that was once raging in Alaska,[110] away from his island. The power of the third one was a gift of extraordinary clairvoyance. Generally speaking, every shaman differs from all others by virtue of a certain skill, which depends on his possession of a special *yéik* or such equipment that gives him the power to perform certain miracles. One Chilkat shaman is said to have owned a mask with one side hard as stone and the other as soft as wood can possibly be. This mask had the power to attract the same *takiek* [*daagi yéigi?*] that had dared to fly to the river Nass to find Yéil's palace. One side of its face and of the whole body turned into stone when it hit Yéil's palace, but it remains alive and helps brave warriors in their raids and various other adventures.[111]

Shamans occupy an important and honorable place in society, especially among their kin and clan relatives. In the past, when Tlingit villages were almost inaccessible to the white man, the shaman's *barabora* occupied an honorable place among other *baraboras*. But since the time when the Russian colonial government and the American officers and civil officials began persecuting shamans, they started to live in remote places, isolated from human habitat.

A terrible persecutor of shamans in Alaska was the captain of a military boat stationed in Sitka, Mr. Glass.[112] Hunting shamans was his favorite pastime and sport. A captured shaman was usually invited aboard his boat and received with honor. Glass talked to him in a friendly manner, inquiring about his life, the number of his *yéik*, the extent of their strength and power, etc. Then he would announce that he was also a shaman who owned yéik and suggested that they compete against each other. Upon his order, a charged electric battery was brought out. The shaman was asked to hold the wires in his hands, while the two poles were being connected. The shaman's body began to twist. His own people, witnessing his strange and funny poses and hearing screams and moans, became frightened. The shaman himself learned a practical lesson about the power of his white colleague. But the captain did not stop at that. Shamans always left his boat with their heads half shaved and covered with oil paint, and having promised not to practice shamanism any more.

Of course, such harsh measures discouraged many shamans but did not totally destroy this occupation in Alaska. The truth of the matter is that shamanism not only brings honor and inspires respectful fear but is very profitable as well. Sometimes shamans receive large piles of blankets for their services. Despite the enormous efforts of Christianity to eradicate paganism among the southeastern Alaskan Indians, some shamans still practice there. One of them from the Killisnoo area is probably still alive, and at least five more can be found in isolated villages.*[113]

The duties of a shaman vary according to local conditions and different times. They could be very broad and complicated as it used to be in large settlements in the days of old, or could be limited to fortune-telling and curing as they are today. In most cases, in the old days of paganism, a shaman would only serve one clan or one tribe. Rarely would two or three neighboring, related, or friendly clans use his services. In the latter case, the shaman had to possess an enormous prestige and to be of noble origin. The shaman's relationship with his own clan was characterized by special duties. The life of the clan was strongly influenced by its shaman. Before any undertaking, the clan turned to its shaman for advice. Let us say, a new hunting and fishing season arrived, e.g., during the month of March, herring came close to shore to spawn. (Herring eggs are a favorite Tlingit dish.) Before going out to collect herring eggs, the clan turned to the shaman and asked him to perform, so that, with the help of his yéik, he would chase away bad weather that brings cold air, storms, rains and all other phenomena that interfere with collecting and preparing fish eggs for the entire next year. The same type of performances took place before hunting marine animals (sea otters, hair seals, beavers), bears, and land otters; prior to the arrival of the fish at the shores; before going on a war raid and after returning from it. These were public or clan performances, so to speak, where the entire clan was present and for which the shaman received a payment from that group—a certain portion of the catch or of the military booty.

However, the shaman's fame and profit depended not only on this type of shamanism. There were other kinds of performances, the private ones in which the shaman with his yéik acted as a curer of the sick. Although curing was not always his duty, he was invariably called to visit a patient in order to determine the nature of the illness and point out its cause. Tlingit believe that witchcraft is the cause of various diseases. Consequently, in such cases, shamanistic perform-ance consists of pointing out the person who has bewitched the patient. Since witches or *nakws'aati* occupy a very important place in Tlingit life, they deserve a special discussion.[114]

We should remember that in medieval Europe and even today in the remote corners of our own motherland inhabited by illiterate people, beliefs in witches and sorcerers persist, e.g., that their black magic can cause bad weather or that their disgusting potions, incantations, and charms can bewitch a person, make him sad, insane, or bring any kind of spiritual or physical affliction. Similarly, Tlingit also believe in the existence of many people who know the secret of witchcraft. Like the European sorcerers who can turn into a pig or a black dog, Indian witches are believed to be able to fly in the air. The favorite destination of their flying journeys is the cemetery. Here they dig in the graves, plucking eyes out of corpses, tearing out their hearts and parts of other internal organs. If no human corpses are available, they find the remains of birds, dogs, wild animals, etc. Witches need corpses not only to obtain substances for their magical practices but to place into them the bewitched objects taken from those whom they wish to harm. One of the most common methods of bewitching consists in obtaining some food or clothing of the victim, or his hair, fingernails, spittle, and so forth, and then placing it inside the corpse of a human being or a dog, after pronouncing a special magic formula. As the corpse rots and deterio-rates, so would the body part from which these objects have been taken. For example, if some hair is taken, the victim's head would ache; in the case of food, his internal organs would rot, etc. This method of witchcraft strongly resembles an old Russian belief in "taking out and burning a footprint or a portrait" of the person whom the witch wishes to kill.[115]

Another method of harming the victim is to give him some bewitched potion to drink or food to eat. Tlingit Indians strongly believe in witchcraft as well as in magical cures from its effects. Hence, the *nakws'aati* is both their spiritual advisor and curer of bodily afflictions. Their belief in witchcraft being both the cause of illness and its cure seems quite natural. The one who knows how to cause a disease should also know how to cure it.[116] With their superstitions and a very limited understanding of the laws of nature and the phenomena of the spiritual life, the Tlingit tend to attribute all illnesses to witchcraft. Whether a person's arm or leg stops functioning as a result of a prolonged rheumatism, or whether he begins to spit blood and then develops consumption—all of this is believed to have been caused by a *nakws'aati*, as revenge for an insult or upon the request of others.

There have been, of course, some cases of illness being caused by eating a significant amount of some abominable stuff offered by a witch, such as a dried and powdered piece of a corpse or something like that, which can poison the blood and make one ill. When such cases were revealed, they only strengthened the superstitions of the savages and made them even more superstitious. Therefore the Tlingit fear witchcraft more than anything else in the world. On the other hand, there is nothing more shameful and insulting than being called a "*nakws'aatí.*" This is tantamount to being accused of the most terrible crimes. The accused had to defend himself in front of all the people, otherwise his closest relative would repudiate him. It is true, however, that if the suspect's relatives belong to a large and populous *barabora*, while the accuser, on the contrary, is weak and poor, he would fear revenge and would not dare to pronounce the terrible word "*nakws'aatí*" in public.

Usually, when witchcraft has been revealed, the shaman's participation is indispensable. As soon as somebody develops a serious illness, other members of the family organize a council and decide whether to invite a shaman to visit the patient. If the shaman lives far away and does not want to come, they go to him with or without the patient. If the shaman is invited to the house, the usual order of the invitation is the following. In the evening or early in the morning, one of the closest relatives of the patient goes to the shaman's *barabora* and, before entering it, calls the shaman from the outside, "*o, igukkhuat!*" [possibly *i gúkx woo.aat*]. The shaman pretends not to understand what is going on and orders this cry to be repeated three more times."[117] Only after that is the time of his seance set up. If the shaman lives far away and does not want to visit the patient's house, relatives of the latter gather several blankets and other gifts and bring them to the shaman's *barabora*. These *barabora*s are always located somewhere along the shore, deep inside a quiet, beautiful inlet, away from people, but easily accessible by canoe. At the present time, however, shamans are moving away from inlets, deep into the forest. They often have two or three such special *barabora*s, plus a house in the village."[118]

The performance of shamanistic rituals and other related activities differ, depending on the specific circumstances under which they take place. They could be more solemn and elaborate, demanding greater physical efforts and agility of movement on the part of the shaman. But they could also be modest and brief, or unusually wild and hysterical, or could be limited almost entirely to funny tricks and entertainment of the audience. The most interesting are the shamanistic performances aimed at helping the patient by finding out the nature of witchcraft and pointing out the witch. A large *barabora* with a fireplace in the middle is always selected for such a performance [*radenie*]."[119] A large fire is built and the patient is laid on furs near it. The shaman arrives with his paraphernalia and assistants-singers, and puts on his ceremonial attire. He does that behind a partition or in a distant corner of the *barabora*. On his head he puts a hat made of marten or ermine skins, with several reeds sticking out. Several straps of hide are tightly tied around his half-naked body and over his shoulders and hips. He remains barefoot or wears light moccasins. In his hand, the shaman always holds a wooden rattle, usually with a figure of some bird carved on it. Sometimes he ties to each of his arms a fan (a bird wing) that can be folded and unfolded any time.

Gradually the *barabora* is filled up with relatives of the patient and visitors. In a dignified manner, all of them quietly take their seats—women with women, and men with men. The singers and drummers usually paint their faces with various designs, tie kerchiefs around their heads and, like everyone else in the *barabora*, wrap *naaxein* or blankets around their shoulders. They start beating the drums in a rhythmic and solemn fashion. The shaman, standing above the patient, slowly starts his monotonous and wild ritual song, the singers join in, and the shaman begins his performance. The words of the song are difficult to make out, one hears only such sounds, as "go-go-go," "gi-gi-gi," repeated after equal intervals. At first the shaman dances in one place, making convulsive movements with his arms and legs. He rolls his eyes and fixes them permanently on one particular spot, as if peering at something, vigorously shakes his head and body, and so forth. Then he begins running in circles around the fire. The drums are being beaten faster and faster, the songs change and their tempo increases. The fire is now reaching up high, its broken flames menacingly lighting the *barabora* and the painted faces of the savages. The shaman performs incredible jumps. As if driven by an unnatural force, he has already jumped over the fire several times and has changed several masks and rattles. Occasionally deafening wild sounds and words escape from his mouth. He has already stopped near and bent over the patient several times, but each time jumped back as if thrown by an invisible force. One more terrible jump, one more wild cry, and scarlet blood begins gushing out of the shaman's mouth with every deep breath. One more convulsive movement and he falls on his knees in front of the patient's bed, stretching his arms into the air, as if trying to catch and hold something. This is usually the end of the performance. The exhausted shaman is approached by his assistants and relatives who give him a few sips of salt water which gradually makes the flow of blood stop. At that time or a little later, the shaman announces the name of the person who has bewitched the patient, describes the methods used by the witch and says what has to be done to cure the patient. The work of the shaman usually ends at this point.

Next evening the shaman's [patient's] relatives gather for another meeting, where they decide how to reward the shaman and what to do about the witch. The shaman usually receives a pile of blankets. If the *nakws'aati* belongs to a noble clan and a large family, he is simply asked to "lower the sickness to the bottom of the sea," but if he is poor and has nobody to defend him, he is caught and "tied up."

"Lowering the illness to the bottom of the sea" consists of the following. A messenger is secretly sent to the person believed to be responsible for the illness, and he humbly pleads with the witch to have pity on the patient and drown the substance used in witchcraft. Of course, the imaginary or the true culprit denies everything, but sometimes, because of ambition or the desire to keep his enemies in fear, he admits knowing the cause of the illness. He says that somebody else is the actual witch, but that he does know where the unclean substance is buried, and agrees to lower it to the bottom of the sea. Such confessions are rarely made, except maybe by overly ambitious, stupid people, or by very close relatives of the patient.

Most often the *nakws'aati* does not admit his guilt and then, even if he happens to be an influential person, the patient's relatives use force to make him confess. Having found a convenient moment, for example, when the *nakws'aati* goes hunting to an isolated place in his canoe, the conspirators attack him and tie his arms and legs with thin straps of hide or sinew. Then they carry him to some secluded spot—an abandoned fisherman's *barabora* or hut, or simply an uninhabited island. There they tie him to something and set up a constant watch near him. The tied-up witch is not allowed to eat, drink, lie down, or sleep in order to force him to confess sooner. If the *nakws'aati* finally admits his guilt, he has to carry out the complete ceremony of "lowering the substance into the water," with the guardsmen watching him.

But if he does not confess, they torture him with hunger and thirst, until he is so exhausted that nothing but a skeleton remains. Most tied-up witches die of exhaustion, or are drowned and killed. A *nakws'aati* is often taken to one of those underwater rocks that become totally dry during low tide but are completely covered during high tide. One could imagine the water rising higher and higher from the feet of the doomed witch to his knees, then up to his waist and higher, and finally there is no longer any possibility of fighting the waves. The ground slips away from his feet, the drowning person tries to swim, but the sea is infinite and a human being cannot fight this powerful element. Just picturing this scene makes one's hair stand on end. And what about the feelings of the poor, exhausted *nakws'aati* during these few hours! In some cases the witch used to be placed in a box and buried alive.

Occasionally very young boys and girls were accused of witchcraft and tied up. In the old days, they were rarely rescued. Under the Russians, witches found refuge in the fort [Novoarkhangel'sk] and remained there forever. At the present time, relatives of a *nakws'aati* try to appeal secretly to the police, if such can be found nearby. Not infrequently visiting fur traders and merchants, informed by these relatives, defended the unfortunate ones and came to their rescue.

Nevertheless, even nowadays, many helpless witches, young and old, lose their lives. Rumors about their deaths arrive too late. The Alaskan court handles numerous trials involving murders and mutilations of witches. The guilty persons are severely punished, but this does not persuade the Indians to abandon such practices. And it will take a long time, before the light of truth drives away the darkness of pagan superstitions.

Anatolii Kamenskii: Tlingit Indians of Alaska

KAMENSKII'S ANNOTATION

1. See annotation from the summary of the author's presentation of Iroquois social life and religion as described by Morgan in *Ancient Society.*

2. See V. Solov'ev, Collected Works, vol. VI, 1901, pp. 158-165, for a characterization and refutation of these theories.

3. *Siukli* or bunches of little bones [shells] [*kostiashki*] strung on a thread were brought from elsewhere. The little bones themselves are oblong sticks, about one and one-half inches long, somewhat sharp on one end, strongly resembling large porcupine quills with their points cut off. Under the Russians, the *siukli* were widely used by all natives. At the present time, however, they have not completely lost their value only among the natives of the interior of Alaska, such as the *Kolchane* [Kolchan], the *Mednovtsy* [Lower Ahtna and Eyak], and others.

4. This name originates from the word *kanu*—"to sit" and *ka* [*ḵáa*] or *kha*— "man," and means—"The Sitting One." Whether this was a male or female, myths do not tell, but more likely it was a male, an old man, "eternally sitting."

5. According to another version, this happened in the following way. Once upon a time Kitkukhinsi was sitting on the beach and noticed a large school of killer whales passing by very close to the shore. One of the killer whales started a conversation with the inconsolable mother. Having learned that childlessness was the cause of the woman's sorrow, the killer whale advised her to find a black pebble on the bottom of the sea and swallow it. She followed the advice: went into the water, found the pebble (according to another version of the story, the killer whale itself gave it to her), swallowed it, washed it down with sea water, and became pregnant.

6. According to another version of the story, the uncle took Yéil far out to sea and threw him overboard in order to drown him. Yéil, however, with the help of the killer whales, was able to walk to the shore along the bottom of the sea and reappeared at his uncle's house.

7. According to another version, Yéil revived several dead boys; the cause of their death, however, is not mentioned.

8. The same myth is told among the *Kenaitsy* [Tanaina] living in the vicinity of Kenaiskii Bay [Cook Inlet]. It appears even though there is no *saak* either in Kenaiskii Bay or in any other location close to the territory of the *Kenaitsy*. This

myth glorifies Yéil not so much for having taught mankind to obtain fire from wood, but for giving them the *saak*-fish considered by the Indians to be a very tasty and expensive dish. The little fish is no more than a quarter of an *arshin* long and resembles smelt *[koriushka]*. Every year it comes close to the shores of one of the Chilkat area inlets in huge numbers. It is very greasy and tasty. The Indians dry, smoke or salt it, and enjoy eating it prepared in any of these ways.

9. Mt. Edgecumbe—a volcano not totally inactive—is located on the island bearing the same name [Kruzof Island] near the Island of Sitka [Baranof Island].

10. The belief that hell is a terribly cold place and that the soul's torments there consist of living in constant cold, without a chance of getting warm, is widespread among some of the tribes of the wild North. In connection with this, by the way, there is a story about one missionary proselytizing in the Far North [Siberia?]. He often tried to frighten his rather sinful flock with the fire of hell, but during such sermons, would always see satisfaction and happiness, instead of fear, on the faces of his listeners. He did not fail to complain to his bishop about that sad phenomenon. The bishop, however, immediately understood what sort of hell should have been used to scare the northerners. When the time had come to preach to the fearless sinners, smiling even at the description of the terrible tortures of hell, the bishop threatened them with such a hell where frost would be a hundred times stronger than the one they had to endure on earth. He succeeded in achieving his goal—not a single person wished to go to such a hell.

Anatolii Kamenskii: Tlingit Indians of Alaska

TRANSLATOR'S ANNOTATIONS

*1. The use of the term "savage" (Russian *dikar'*) here and elsewhere is not derogatory and follows Morgan's scheme of the evolution of human society.

*2. Reid, Thomas Mayne (1818-1883), an English writer, author of romantic adventure stories about American Indians. His books were extremely popular in Russia in the nineteenth and the early twentieth centuries, especially among the younger readers.

*3. The author is mistaken, thinking that Sherlock Holmes was an American.

*4. "Central Indian Desert" refers to the deserts of Utah and Nevada.

*5. "Insular Indians" refers to the Indians of the Pacific Northwest Coast.

*6. The author's brief summary of Morgan's presentation of Iroquois culture omitted from this translation is fairly accurate. He mentions the evolution of the social organization from the gens to the tribal confederacy. Peace and war chiefs are discussed, and so is the matrilineal principle of succession to office. The nature of property owned by tribes and the decision-making process on the tribal level are also mentioned. The significance of blood feud, and especially collective responsibility of kinship groups, are emphasized. Iroquois religion is outlined, with the focus on nature worship and elements of polytheism (among the more advanced tribes). The fact that the Iroquois allegedly acknowledged the existence of the Great Spirit and the Evil Spirit, along with numerous secondary spirits, is emphasized. Idol worship among some of the tribes, as well as the belief in the immortality of the soul and the afterlife are mentioned. Finally Iroquois shamanism (i.e., Medicine Lodges) is described in considerable detail. Despite Kamenskii's insistence on the similarity between the Iroquois and the Tlingit cultures, the material he selected from *Ancient Society* does not support his argument. Nevertheless, his evolutionary views and the conviction that all American Indians shared a similar culture prevented him from seeing essential differences.

*7. Ebrard, Johannes H. A. (1818-1888), German theologian, historian of religion. Author of the *Apologetik. Wissenschaftliche Rechtfertigung des Christenthums*, 1874-75, Vols. I-II.

*8. La Grasserie, Raoul Robert Guerin de (1839-1914), French writer, lawyer, linguist, ethnologist. Author of several works on comparative grammar, and a study entitled *On the Psychology of Religions* (1899), which seems to be the work referred to by Kamenskii.

*9. The reference here is to Solov'ev's article "Primitive Paganism, Its Living and Dead Remnants" ["Pervobytnoe iazychestvo, ego zhivye i mertvye ostatki"], published in 1890. In this paper, Max Muller's concept of "naturism" or nature worship, and E. B. Tylor's theory of animism are criticized as being one-sided and failing to explain the complex process of the origin of religion. Solov'ev himself argued, in this and other works, that the earliest form of religion was "vague monotheism," with an absence of clear distinction between spirits of the dead and deified natural phenomena, other spirits and so forth. This "vague monotheism" or "vague pandemonism" was later on replaced by polytheism. Solov'ev's position seemed close to Kamenskii's own views on the subject, presented in this book. See also V. Solov'ev "Mythological Process in Ancient Paganism" ["Mifologicheskii protsess v drevnem iazychestve"], Collected Works, vol. I, pp. 1-25, 1901.

*10. *Kaliuzhi* or *Koloshi*—the name given to the Tlingit by the Russians was probably derived from the labrets (Russian *kaluzhki*) worn by Tlingit women. While Father Anatolii and his missionary colleagues working in Alaska after its purchase by the United States were aware of the term "Tlingit," they continued to use the old term "Koloshi."

*11. While archaeologists have not been able yet to establish the time of the Tlingit arrival in southeastern Alaska, it undoubtedly occurred earlier than Fr. Anatolii suggested.

*12. While a number of Russian, British and Spanish expeditions sailed along the coast inhabited by the Tlingit in the eighteenth century, the first direct contact occurred between La Perouse and the Lituya Bay Tlingit in 1786, followed by Dixon in 1787, W. Douglas in 1788, and Malaspina in 1791. The first documented Russian contact was probably that of Ismailov and Bocharov in 1788 (see de Laguna 1972:108-180; Gunther 1972:139-182; Emmons 1911).

*13. Americans were called "Waashdan Kwáan," "Boston tribe" or "people of Boston."

*14. The first Russian settlement and fort built among the Tlingit was not in Sitka but in Yakutat; constructed in 1796 it was named Novorossiisk and was destroyed by the Tlingit in 1805 (see Tikhmenev 1978:43-44; de Laguna 1972:166-176).

*15. The author seems to be confusing the Tlingit with interior Athabaskan Indians.

*16. It is more likely that the Tlingit were fighting the Chugach Eskimos rather than the Aleuts (see de Laguna 1972:213).

*17. For a detailed discussion and illustrations of aboriginal Tlingit weaponry see Ratner-Shternberg 1930; see also de Laguna 1972:585-592; Krause 1970:145-146.

*18. According to information obtained by de Laguna (1972:412- 413) in Yakutat, copper was known to the Tlingit prior to European arrival and was obtained through trade with the Copper River Ahtna. It was used for making knives, scrapers, arrowheads as well as ornaments. It was considered quite valuable.

*19. For more details see Khlebnikov's biography of Baranov (Khlebnikov 1973:8-9).

*20. The drum was used by the shaman who accompanied his kinsmen in a war party.

*21. With the possible exception of some wealthy aristocrats (heads of houses and clans), most Tlingit men performed a variety of daily chores. Slave labor did not constitute an important source of labor (de Laguna 1972:469-475).

*22. Fathers rarely administered these cold baths to young boys, instead it was the prerogative of their maternal uncles, i.e., their senior matrilineal relatives.

*23. *"shkat"*—possibly a typographic error; more likely *"ishkat,"* bags and baskets made of plant fibers by the natives of Siberia and the Aleutian Islands (Dr. Lydia Black, personal communication).

*24. A number of observers (e.g., Krause 1970:92-93) as well as my own Tlingit consultants confirmed these suggestions.

*25. Many Russian and other European and American observers shared this view: the Tlingit were perceived as more independent and vain than Aleuts, Athabaskans, and Eskimos. Among the reasons for this view could have been their more complex organization and material culture, aggressive trading habits, or facial features that appeared less Mongoloid (cf. Veniaminov 1886:631-641).

*26. *Lingít x'éináx* means "in the Tlingit language," as in *"Wáa sá duwasáakw yáat'aa Lingít x'éináx?"* ("what is this called in Tlingit?").

*27. This is probably a confusion with the term "guttural."

*28. The author's description of the Tlingit language is rather simplistic; for a more sophisticated earlier Russian description see Veniaminov 1846.

*29. "Tribe" (Russian *plemia*) refers to matrilineal exogamous moieties. The Tlingit themselves have frequently used the English term "tribe" to refer to these social categories.

*30. *"Barabora"* (Russian term for any native house in Siberia and North America) refers here to the large winter house of a matrilineage, subdivided into extended matrilineal families or sublineages, which the author calls "families" (Russian *"semeistvo"*).

*31. This statement may reflect the views of the author's informants belonging to the Raven moiety or his own conclusions drawn from the fact that the Raven was believed to be the creator of the universe.

*32. This is clearly a Sitka bias—there the Kiks.ádi clan was considered to be the founder of the village and, hence, its original owner. The term "Khikhchaty" seems to be the author's own invention based on the Tlingit word for frog (*xíxch'*)—the crest of the Kiks.ádi clan. The correct name "Kiks.ádi" is derived from a geographical feature called "Kiks."

*33. Coho salmon was the main crest of the L'uknax.ádi clan; they also claimed the sea lion and had a Sea Lion House in Sitka; the Kiks.ádi clan, however, claimed the cry of the sea lion (Swanton 1908:417). The owl or its cry was claimed by the Kiks.ádi (ibid.). According to my own sources in Sitka, it was claimed primarily by the Clay House (S'é Hít) of the Sitka Kiks.ádi. De Laguna (1972:452) says that it was claimed by another clan of the Raven moiety, the Kwáashk'i Kwáan of Yakutat. Kamenskii seems to have confused clan crests with crests of individual houses/lineages.

*34. Another statement reflecting the Sitka bias of the author's data: the Kaag-waantaan was the leading clan of the Wolf moiety in Sitka and a few other villages but not throughout the entire Tlingit nation. "Kukhantan" may be either the Russian corruption of "Kaagwaantaan" or a rendering of "Kóok Hít Taan," a clan closely related to Kaagwaantaan, also from Sitka; sometimes it is perceived as a lineage of the Kaagwaantaan clan. Veniaminov (1886:577) also used both terms.

*35. Under normal circumstances the youngest nephew would not be the successor.

*36. Only members of a clan, and not the entire village, could take part in the election of a clan chief.

*37. Although there are no other accounts available to verify the author's description of the election of a clan chief, it appears quite plausible (cf. Averkieva 1960:25).

*38. He distributed wealth among members of the opposite moiety who acted as witnesses of his installation as a new chief.

*39. See Appendix, passim.

*40. While the Russian-American Company did play a certain role in the decline of slave sacrifices in Sitka, it had virtually no control over other Tlingit communities. Even in Sitka, slaves were still sacrificed occasionally even after the sale of Alaska in 1867.

*41. "Kachekh-deikeenaa"; according to Jeff Leer (personal communication), this should probably be spelled *Kaajeexdakeen.aa*, lit. "one that (habitually) flies into people's possession," although this word has not been specifically attested. The author's Russian gloss "Pereletnyi" ("the one that flies over") may be correct.

*42. Northern Tlingit villages did not have many free-standing totem poles in front of their houses. More often there were painted house fronts and wooden panels with carved figures of lineages and clan crests. The latter were kept inside the houses and displayed outside during potlatches. This was done in Sitka as late as in 1904, when the Kaagwaantaan had a big potlatch there.

*43. While written certificates and gifts from Europeans, and especially the Russians, were highly valued by the Tlingit and were passed on through the maternal line, they did not replace traditional crest objects. Russian shields, medals, military uniforms and other such objects were probably perceived by the Tlingit as ceremonial artifacts of European chiefs and, hence, owning them indicated high status in the native social hierarchy.

*44. "Copper cannon" should say *"copper hand-loaded cannon"* (Russ. *ruchnaia pushka*), a small-calibre weapon (Dr. Lydia Black, personal communication).

*45. The author's description of American tourists as citizens of a "free" country has an ironic tone, typical of his general attitude toward the American political system, which he compared unfavorably with his own country's Orthodox monarchy.

*46. The man was probably a famous chief of the Deisheetaan clan of the Angoon/Killisnoo area, named Kichnal, Killisnoo Jake or Saginaw Jake. Born in the 1840s, he was baptized in the Russian Church in Sitka in 1887 and given the name Nikolai. He became a native policeman in Killisnoo and was frequently photographed there wearing his policeman's uniform or other regalia. He was also a marshal in the Russian church in Killisnoo, while his lineage house in Angoon (Shdéen Hít) was frequently used for religious Orthodox meetings. Kichnal died in 1908.

*47. The author is probably exaggerating the power of the Tlingit aristocrats in aboriginal times. Wealthy chiefs were uncommon. In fact, special treatment given to certain aristocrats ("chiefs") by Europeans as well as new sources of wealth made available after their arrival might have increased the power and wealth of the native aristocracy.

*48. While it is true that the Russian-American Company treated Tlingit leaders with considerable deference, American authorities also relied on them, especially during the first decades after the purchase of Alaska. In fact, contrary to Kamenskii's statement, chiefs of the major Sitka clans were the first Indian policemen. At the same time, the more democratic and the more powerful Americans did pay less attention to the indigenous system of rank than the Russians who needed all the support they could get and whose own social system was based on a hierarchy of separate estates.

*49. Tlingit kinship terms are always used with a possessive pronoun.

*50. Conflicts between clans and houses of the same moiety were fairly common, despite the ideology of matrilineal solidarity. On the one hand, there was competition over shared crests, and, on the other, a lack of elaborate ritualized forms of settling disputes, in contrast to those used to resolve conflicts between groups belonging to the two opposite moieties.

*51. The account of the conflict between the Kiks.ádi and the L'uknax.ádi is correct in its major details and was probably based on the author's own observations, interviews, and reports in the local newspapers. However, Kamenskii's explanation of the reason for the L'uknax.ádi claims on the frog crest is incorrect (see de Laguna 1972:288-291). Most native accounts suggest that the two clans based their claims on two *different* origin myths. Their use of the same crest was tolerated until the L'uknax.ádi settled in Sitka and began competing with the Kiks.ádi over wealth, power and influence. For additional information, see *Daily Alaska Dispatch*, 2/19/1901; 10/14/1901; 2/10/1903; also see *The Home Mission Monthly*, vol. 17, no. 8:179-180, 1903.

*52. While the author's own description of crest objects and totem poles makes it clear that these were used primarily as heraldic devices, he frequently refers to them as "idols," suggesting a contradiction between his ethnographic observations and missionary bias. For a missionary the "Frog Case" was a perfect illustration of the danger of "paganism," i.e., human lives were "sacrificed" for the sake of the "frog idol."

*53. For details on the origin and history of the L'uknax.ádi and their crests, see de Laguna 1972:23-291.

*54. This was probably taken from one of the newspaper accounts of the event.

*55. In this matrilineal system, a woman's husband and father belong to the same moiety.

*56. The imagination of the author seems to have colored this description.

*57. For a more detailed and accurate account of this feud, see Olson 1967:78-79; Tikhmenev 1978:353. The most detailed account based on years of close contact with the Tlingit is a manuscript entitled "Tlingit War Lasting about 95 Years" written by Fr. Andrei Kashevarov of Juneau and located in the Alaska State Historical Library, Juneau. The war was not between all of Sitka and all Stikine Tlingit, but between specific clans from these two as well as several other communities. Peace was finally established in 1918.

*58. Instead of an evolution from one type of wealth used as a medium of exchange to another, there was a coexistence of all of them.

*59. *Naaxein* referred to Chilkat blankets only; blankets for wearing were called *x'óow* and button blankets—*kaa yooka.bot' x'óow* (see de Laguna 1972:431-444).

*60. This is an interesting piece of evidence not found in other accounts of Tlingit methods of settling disputes (cf. Olson 1967:17-18; Oberg 1937). Distribution of gifts by the injured person among his own clan relatives could also indicate wiping out shame vis-á-vis his own matrilineal kin.

*61. This seems to be a mistake; once an exchange of gifts between the two parties had taken place, there could no longer be any expectations of further compensation.

*62. This myth about an incest between siblings is probably the same as the myth about Xeitl and Haayeeshaanák'u (see Chapter VII below; cf. also Veniaminov 1886:587-588).

*63. For more details on the marriage ceremony, see Veniaminov 1886:617-619; de Laguna 1972:525-527; Olson 1967:18-19; Swanton 1908:428.

*64. This is an example of the Russian missionaries' anti-Presbyterian/anti-American sentiment. While Kamenskii is correct about the Orthodox Church's more negative attitude toward divorce, he fails to mention the fact that Orthodox Tlingit were as reluctant to marry in the Church as their Presbyterian tribesmen. The reason for this was their fear that the "white man's" marriage would become a justification for patrilineal descent and inheritance and hence would undermine the traditional social structure. See the Alaska Church Collection for numerous Russian missionaries' complaints about the Tlingit reluctance to accept the sacrament of marriage until the 1900s-1910s.

*65. The author's explanation of Tlingit "generosity" as being the result of their "vanity" shows his misunderstanding of native culture and a very negative attitude toward the potlatch and the distribution of gifts.

*66. Dikée Aankáawu, literally "chief of the above," was a term and a concept introduced by the missionaries, most likely those of the Orthodox Church. While there probably existed some indigenous notions about a guardian spirit associated with every human being (ax kinaayéigi, "my spirit above") and a common sacred destiny of all the members of a matrilineal clan (shagóon), which in some contexts was personified and appealed to, the kind of monotheism that Kamenskii describes did not seem to have existed. The missionary simply "discovered" a phenomenon he had expected to be there. His description of the Tlingit Heaven resembles Christian Paradise. Earlier Russian sources, such as Veniaminov (1886), fail to mention any supreme deity and so do not use the term Dikée Aankáawu. Instead Veniaminov (1846:42) uses the Tlingit expression haa shagóon ("our destiny") to translate the christian "God." The term Dikée Aankáawu appears in Orthodox prayers translated into Tlingit in the 1890s (or earlier) and published by Donskoi (1895) and Nadezhdin (1896). Presbyterian missionaries also used this term; see also Olson 1967:110; de Laguna 1972:815-816.

*67. Kamenskii himself admits that the Tlingit knew little about the Dikée Aankáawu. His reference to such mythological protagonists as Yéil, Ganook, etc. as "gods" is incorrect but makes sense in light of his theory of primitive religion (see Chapter V).

*68. According to Jeff Leer (personal communication), "there could well be an etymological connection between "ganook" and the verb (singular) "sits," stem "-nook." Fr. Anatolii's interpretation may be at least in part correct, although the particulars may be more complex (e.g., the bird may have been named after its habit of sitting on rocks out at sea, just as the mythical character was "sitting" on an island when Raven stole the water).

*69. By referring to Ganook and other mythical beings as "titans," the author suggests that they preceded Yéil as the Greek titans preceded the Olympic gods.

*70. Visvakarman (Sanskrit: "all accomplishing"); in Hindu mythology, the architect of the gods. The name was originally used as an epithet of any powerful god but later came to personify creative power. Visvakarman is a divine carpenter and master craftsman; he revealed the sciences of architecture and mechanics to man.

*71. According to Veniaminov (1886:590f), "The Kolosh think that there was a time when the earth was not located in its present place but somewhere else, while some other planet occupied its present location. Eventually the two changed places and the present order was established."

*72. The "liver of the world" is mentioned by Swanton (1908:452) and Veniaminov (1886:590); the latter recorded the term for it: *Haayeetl'óogu;* "the liver under (i.e., supporting) us" (Jeff Leer, personal communication). An alternative interpretation of the Russian spelling could be either l'óoxk'oo" ("spawn") or "l'óok'oo" ("murky water"); in other words, the myth may be referring to some kind of spawn or murky water coming from the depths (?) of the earth (Nora Dauenhauer, personal communication).

*73. Naasshagiyéil ("Raven at the head of Nass") is mentioned by Veniaminov (1886:580) simply as the term for the dwelling place of the Raven (Yéil). On the other hand, Swanton's Christianized informant Katishan described Naasshagiyéil as the original being that had created Yéil. In the origin myth recorded by Swanton (1909:80-154) from Katishan he is described as both the wicked uncle of Yéil and the owner of daylight (cf. myths presented by Kamenskii in this chapter). Swanton's Sitka informants did not mention Naasshagiyéil. Katishan might have been trying to systematize the various myths of the Raven cycle (cf. de Laguna 1972:839-844).

*74. No other source mentions this character.

*75. Other versions of the myth of the origin of daylight are reported in Veniaminov 1886:584-587; Swanton 1909:81-83; de Laguna 1972:856, 862.

*76. Raven's struggle with his wicked uncle is described also in Veniaminov 1886:580-584; Swanton 1909:3, 81-82; de Laguna 1972:844-845, 848-849, etc.

*77. The story of the theft of fresh water from Ganook is described also in Veniaminov 1886:587-588; Swanton 1909:4, 83; de Laguna 1972:847, 865, etc.

*78. The myth of X'anaxgaatwaayáa is also reported in de Laguna 1972:865, 867; Swanton 1909:11, 93; Zuboff 1973.

*79. This was not a "castle" but rather a giant box or a house; some contemporary story-tellers refer to it as an "ark."

*80. This song is recorded in Zuboff 1973:12-14 and de Laguna 1972:867.

*81. See Swanton 1909:12-13, 91; de Laguna 1972:868-869.

*82. See Swanton 1909:6-7; Krause 1970:182; de Laguna 1972:868.

*83. This seems to be a Christian influence. It is interesting, however, than an earlier Russian missionary-ethnographer recorded it too (Veniaminov 1886:579-580). Native reinterpretation of the Raven myths in the light of Christianity persists in the 1970s-1980s (Kan MS, 1979-1980). As de Laguna (1972:842) points out: "For those of serious intellectual bent, Raven myths can serve as a bridge between the old traditional ways and the new life, for the mythology is interpreted so that it can be reconciled with the teachings of the mission and thus show that the old-time natives were not unenlightened savages living in darkness, as supercilious whites imagined. Thus Raven sometimes, and for some narrators, appears in noble and impressive guise as the Creator."

*84. Cf. Veniaminov 1886:610-612.

*85. According to Jeff Leer (personal communication), "gus'ɣee" or "gus'k'iɣee" has not been attested alone; "Gus'k'iɣeekwáan" means "people from under (i.e., supporting) the clouds," and was used to refer to the Europeans.

*86. This information was confirmed by one of my Tlingit consultants, Mr. Mark Jacobs, Jr.

*87. According to Veniaminov (1886:611-612), it was Yéil himself who fought with the Old Woman Below over the pole supporting the earth.

*88. An interesting example of imitative magic, not mentioned in other accounts; cf. Veniaminov's (1886:612-613) account of the Tlingit ceremonial behavior during the eclipse of the moon.

*89. Beliefs in Tl'anaxéedákw persisted until recently. See Swanton 1909:365-368; de Laguna 1972:884-885; Kan MS, 1979-1980. Kamenskii seems to have added elements of a Russian (European) folktale to the native myth, although it is possible that this blending of Tlingit and Russian oral traditions had already taken place by the time he recorded the myth; cf. Dauenhauer 1975:123-143. According to Richard Dauenhauer (personal communication), the narrative frame of the story is not Tlingit, it is clearly a retelling.

*90. It is not surprising that Tl'anaxéedákw was identified with the Mother of God: both were represented as a woman with an infant and both brought good fortune.

*91. Once again the author tries to fit the data into his theoretical scheme and, in the process, distorts it. There was never a cult of Yéil or Xeitl, hence there was no "decline" of it either. Whether the Tlingit still believed in these mythological characters is a complex question, but it would seem that, in Kamenskii's times, some Tlingit still took their origin myths very seriously, despite the fact that Christianity was already undermining native cosmology.

*92. The classification of spirits presented here is similar to that of Veniaminov (1886:592-593), but is not confirmed by any of the later ethnographers, such as Swanton, de Laguna and others. It is possible that the Russian missionary ethnographers were adding systematically to the less rigid native beliefs. The spirits were not inherently evil; their actions depended on the shaman's use of them (see Chapter X). Most Tlingit nouns are not normally differentiated for number. Yéik can be singular or plural (tléix' yéik 'one spirit'; déix yéik 'two spirits'); yéikx' is specifically a collective plural '(a group of) spirits.' (Jeff Leer, personal communication).

*93. Kaa yéigi was only one of a number of terms for the human soul (spirit); more common was kaa yakgwahéiyágu.

*94. Keewakáawu was the heaven of slain warriors, translated by Swanton (1908:461) simply as "way up." Veniaminov (1886:592) also mentions it. This was a happy place where warriors dwelled without worries, engaged in games; their movement appeared in the sky as the Northern Lights.

*95. Another example of the influence of Christian eschatology on Kamenskii's ethnography. Diyée Aankáawu—Chief of the Below—was a notion introduced by the missionaries and it never enjoyed much popularity among the Tlingit. The Christian cosmological opposition of the top and the bottom did not make much sense to them. An underground domain for sinners was an alien notion inspired by missionary sermons. S'igeekáawu aaní simply meant the "village of the dead" and was used to refer both to the cemetery and the invisible interior village where the spirits of the dead dwelled; s'igeekáawu means "the dead," literally "the bones' people."

*96. There is no evidence to support this statement; all sources say that human beings were believed to come back as human beings. Contemporary ethnographic observations (de Laguna 1972:776-781; Kan MS, 1979-1980) confirm this.

*97. This was a common aboriginal notion subsequently syncretized with an Orthodox idea of the guardian angel (see de Laguna 1972:812-813; Kan MS, 1979-1980).

*98. On Greenland Eskimo bear ceremonialism, see, for example, Rasmussen (1938:135-138).

*99. See Veniaminov 1886:613-615; Swanton 1909:126-128; de Laguna 1972:880-882; McClellan 1970.

*100. While many Tlingit personal names are derived from those of animals, the reference is to the animal crests of lineages and clans rather than the animals themselves, as the author suggests.

*101. Touching the corpse. a source of great pollution. was dangerous to human beings, especially the matrilineal relatives of the deceased.

*102. While the mourners were the matrilineal relatives of the deceased, his closest female affines. wives and daughters. mourned as well.

*103. According to Swanton (1908:429) and several other sources, the corpse was taken out through an opening in the rear wall of the houses, made by removing a plank.

*104. This is a plausible explanation, although Swanton (1908:429) offered a different one: a live dog was thrown out to confuse the ghost, that is, to make him carry away a dog rather than a human being to the land of the dead.

*105. This practice was quite rare.

*106. For other accounts of the nineteenth century Tlingit funeral, see Veniaminov 1886:622-623; Donskoi 1893:856-857; Krause 1956:156-157; Jones 1914:147-153; Swanton 1908:429-431; Olson 1967:58-60; de Laguna 1972:532-533.

*107. The reference is to an article entitled "The Ancestors of American Indigenes," *American Antiquarian*, January-February, 1902, vol. 24, no. 1, pp. 3-18. Mr. Hallock's hypothesis cannot be supported by ethnographic or historical evidence.

*108. For other descriptions of Tlingit shamanism, see Veniaminov 1886:595-605; de Laguna 1972:669-727; Olson 1967:110-115; Swanton 1908:463-469. Although Kamenskii never quotes Veniaminov, his own account seems to rely heavily on this earliest description of shamanism.

*109. The story seems to have been borrowed from Veniaminov 1886:599-600.

*110. The smallpox epidemic of 1835-1836 devastated Sitka as well as other Tlingit communities; see Veniaminov 1886:641-642; Tikhmenev 1978:198-199.

*111. This episode also seems to have been taken from Veniaminov 1886:600-601.

*112. See Glass (1890) for his own account of his persecution of shamans and other activities aimed at "civilizing" the Tlingit.

*113. Shamans of the Angoon/ Killisnoo area were among the most conservative who resisted American pressure longer than others. The last ones were still practicing there in the 1920s or even the 1930s (Kan MS, 1979-1980).

*114. For other descriptions of Tlingit witchcraft, see Veniaminov 1886:605-609; Swanton 1908:469-472; Olson 1967:115-116; de Laguna 1972:728-744.

*115. This method consisted in "taking out the victim's footprint" and burning it or making a fire on top of the footprint itself. Other operations could be performed on the victim's footprint and portrait in order to harm him. See Tokarev 1957:135.

*116. Witches were not "spiritual advisors" and could not be called "curers" either, since they were forced to undo the evil they had done.

*117. Veniaminov (1886:606) adds that the shaman listened to this cry as if it was a distant, unclear, but familiar voice. He was supposed to hear the voice of the witch in the modulations of the caller's voice. According to Jeff Leer (personal communication), this expression could be *"i gúkx woo.aat,"* 'they have gone in your ear.'

*118. Shamans ordinarily did not dwell in separate houses in the village. The isolated huts mentioned here were either summer dwellings or special places for retreats. No other sources dealing with shamanism mention this.

*119. The use of the term *radenie* is noteworthy, since it illustrates the author's extremely negative attitude toward shamanism. In Russia it was used to refer to rituals of sectarians (Jehovah's Witnesses, Seventh Day Adventists, etc.), seen by the official Orthodox Church as one of its greatest enemies. Such rituals were often accompanied by singing, dancing, trance, and other forms of behavior reminiscent of the shamanistic performance.

Appendix 1

Petition to His Grace Nikolai, Bishop of the Aleutian Islands and Alaska from the Dean of Clergy of the Sitka Parish, Hieromonk Anatolii

(October 27, 1896)

Having found out that there is a vacancy for a priest in the St. Aleksander Nevskii Cathedral in San Francisco, I dare to appeal to Your Grace with a most humble petition to transfer me from Sitka to that position. The following reasons have forced me to bother Your Grace with this appeal. First of all, my presence here is not appropriate because, having become more acquainted with the local conditions of parish life and the Russian Orthodox mission, I am now convinced that a married priest would be more useful in Sitka. He would be able to do the same things for the mission with much less effort than I. Secondly, considering the situation of the parish priest in San Francisco, it would be more appropriate for me to serve there. Thirdly, after only one year of service in Sitka, my health, under the combined influence of the Sitka climate and the conditions of life I am forced to lead because of my work, has become so much worse that it is necessary for me either to leave Sitka for one or two years or to change my way of life completely. The latter, of course, is impossible under the present circumstances. Consequently, I am choosing the former option and hope that, if Your Grace decides to satisfy my appeal, I will, or at least will try to be, as useful in my new position as I am here now.

> Your Grace's Most Humble Servant Hieromonk Anatolii October 27, 1896 [*Library of Congress, Manuscript Division, Alaska Church Collection, B-9*]

Appendix 2

Diocese of Alaska, Office of the Russian Clergy, Sitka, Alaska, February 5, 1891

Certificate

A Hoonah Indian Vasilii Nal'khakou leaving Sitka for Hoonah has asked me to give him a certificate confirming his Orthodoxy. Satisfying his wish, I am witnessing herewith that the above mentioned Indian was baptized by me about two years ago and that, since the day of his baptism, he has shown himself to be a zealous Christian, despite the fact that his parents and all of his relatives are pagans.

Priest of the Sitka St. Michael Cathedral Vladimir Donskoi
[*Alaska State Historical Library, Juneau, Alaska*]

Appendix 3

Diocese of Alaska, Office of the Russian Clergy, Sitka, Alaska

Certificate

A Hoonah Indian Andrei Kendukol' with his entire family numbering ten people has accepted the Orthodox Faith and has been baptized by me. Since the baptism, he has demonstrated his love of Orthodoxy by regular church attendance. His relatives belonging to the Presbyterian heresy abuse him in all sorts of ways, but Kendukol' quietly endures everything for the sake of God's Name. I am giving him this document to encourage his further Christian success and wellbeing; let it remind him of the words of Our Savior who said, "the one that suffered till the end will be saved."

Priest of the Sitka St. Michael Cathedral Vladimir Donskoi, December 6, 1891.

Seal

[*Alaska State Historical Library, Juneau, Alaska*]

Appendix 4

Excerpt from a Report to His Grace Nikolai, Bishop of the Aleutian Islands and Alaska, from the Priest of the Sitka Parish, Fr. Vladimir Donskoi

November 19, 1894

The icon of Christ the Savior intended for the deceased interpreter Mikhail Sinkiel has not been given to anybody yet. I was planning to give it to Sinkiel's widow, but his brothers and relatives are asking me to explain to Your Grace that if the icon is given to her, it will be passed on to her own relatives who belong to a totally different clan (Kaagwaantaan) and do not live in Sitka. Sinkiel's clan, the so-called Kiks.ádi, would then be forced to forget that it had been honored and blessed by the Holy Synod through Sinkiel. Not wishing to incite hostility among the Kolosh, I told them that I will present this case to Your Grace's judgement and will do whatever Your Grace orders me to do. The Kolosh happily agreed to my proposition and promised to obey Your Grace's decision.

> [*Library of Congress, Manuscript Division, Alaska Church Collection, D-432*]

Appendix 5

THE STATUTES
OF THE ARCHANGEL MICHAEL SOCIETY OF
MUTUAL AID
SITKA, ALASKA

January 1, 1896

[The original written in Tlingit and Russian.]

1. Only Sitka residents can be members of the Society.

2. A person wishing to join the Society has to inform the priest about it.

3. The candidate has to make a public pledge in the church that he will obey the following rules:

   a) stop drinking wine;
   b) stop playing cards;
   c) renounce old pagan ceremonies and rituals;
   d) not to participate in other pagan festivities;
   e) avoid quarrels;
   f) not to slander others;
   g) not to bear grudges or carry out revenge against others;
   h) not to believe in spirits of shamans;
   i) not to perform any memorial feasts for the dead.

4. Each member has to pay monthly dues in the amount of 25 cents or pay the entire annual membership in advance.

5. $10.00 is allocated for the burial of a poor member of the Society; a sick member is given from $1.00 to $3.00 per week; help is also provided for poor orphans.

6. Members can participate in memorial dinners [*pominki*]; they are also allowed to receive compensation for their work performed during funerals, but only in cash and not in blankets.

7. Members that have broken these rules two or three times are to be tried by the Society and expelled.

8. Members not paying their dues for six months are deprived of the right to receive assistance.

9. Two members are elected to be in charge of the candles bought by the Society.

10. During the funeral of a member, other members must stand with lighted candles and later accompany the body to the cemetery, still carrying those candles; the candles are purchased by the members themselves.

11. The society has two chief officers: the priest and a person elected from among the Indians.

12. The treasury of the society is kept in the church.

13. Observance of these statutes is monitored by the members themselves.

***

OATH

I promise and swear before the Holy Gospel and the Life-giving Cross that, upon joining the Sitka Brotherhood of St. Mikhail the Archangel, I will obey all the statutes of this society. May God help me in this with all His Might. As a confirmation of my words I am kissing the Cross of My Lord God. Amen.

[Library of Congress, Manuscript Division, Alaska Church Collection, D-322]

Appendix 6

Report to the Right Reverend Nikolai, Bishop of the Aleutian Islands and Alaska, from Hieromonk Anatolii, Dean of Clergy of the Sitka District (January 13/25, 1896)

I have the honor to inform Your Grace about the establishment of the Arch-angel Michael Society of Temperance and Mutual Aid among the Orthodox Kolosh of Sitka. On January 1, 1896, following the Divine Liturgy, seventeen Indians made a vow not to drink wine or perform pagan rituals any more. The formula they used had been prepared beforehand and translated into the Kolosh language. On Thursday, January 4, during the meeting of the Society, its trea-sury was established. In addition to the $10.00 I myself donated for the Society, the amount of initial donations totalled $18.75, which the members decided to give to the church *starosta* [warden] S. I. Kostromitinov for safekeeping. At the present time, members are very much worried about badges. They strongly desire to wear the same badges as those used by members of the Sitka [Russian] Brotherhood. Having nothing against this myself, I promised them to appeal to members of the Russian Brotherhood, so as to find out whether they would agree to supply the members of this new society with their own extra badges, at least temporarily, or whether they would agree to sell them. For that purpose I called for an emergency meeting of the Russian Brotherhood on January 3, at 7 p.m. . . . . Members of the Russian Brotherhood gave a negative answer to the proposal to sell their badges. They also expressed a wish not to allow the Kolosh to own this type of badge, since it would force most members of the Russian Brotherhood to resign. When asked why they would leave the brotherhood, some of them gave the following explanation: "We are neither fools nor Kolosh to wear the same badges; we do not want to be equated with them. We are afraid they might start pushing us in church, because they are so ambitious, etc." Eighteen persons were present at the meeting . . . . Having presented all this information to Your Grace's examination, I would like most humbly to ask for Your orders about the confirmation of the new society and its statutes, attached herewith, as well as about the badges for its members. It would have been desirable, whether Your Grace would decide to allow the members of the tem-perance society to wear the old brotherhood badges or whether You would institute a new uniform, to have the badges sent here in the near future. In addition, it would have been desirable, to have a government stamp with an appropriate seal depicted on it. Otherwise the Kolosh, with their great weakness for all kinds of decorations, will be abusing them and there would be no way to stop such abuses without the authority of the government. In addition, if the badges are approved by the government, the Temperance Society will acquire greater authority in the eyes of the natives as well as the whites. Initially badges without the stamp would suffice. About thirty to forty are needed. Some additional ones might be required in a couple of months. I hope that the Sitka Society will soon have a chapter in Juneau, Killisnoo and other places inhabited by the [Tlingit] Indians.

> Your Grace's
> Most Humble Servant
> The Dean of Clergy of the
> Sitka District
> Hieromonk Anatolii

January 13/25, 1896

Sitka, Alaska

[*Library of Congress, Manuscript Division, Alaska Church Collection, D-322*]

Appendix 7

Letters to His Grace Nikolai, Bishop of the Aleutian Islands and Alaska, from Orthodox Tlingit Leaders of Sitka, Members of the Indian Brotherhood of St. Michael

January 23, 1896

I. During Your last visit, I was introduced to You by Fr. Vladimir. You were kind enough to ask my name and gave me some good advice. This was five years ago. I promised you to attend church and sing in the choir. I have strictly obeyed that promise. And now with God's help I have joined the Society. I have been hearing about it for a long time, but never hoped to live to be its member. I have a great desire to see You. If, however, God does not grant this, I ask for your blessing and Your prayers for me.

Member of the Society Jacob P. Kanagood /his own signature/

———————————————————————————————

II. Since the very day I joined the Society, I am happy and have only one wish: to see Your Grace and to have You see me and other members of the Society. For the time being, You can see my own name and the names of others that have signed this letter. I am asking You to pray for me and for them, and for the growth and increase of the Society. I promise to keep the pledges I have made formally.

Nikifor Kul'kita [+]

I would like to tell You what I and others are feeling at this moment. The word You have spoken during Your last visit here was understood and not forgotten. We are serving the Church loyally, and our society is the proof of that. Thanks to God, it now numbers seventeen people. We have decided to abandon all our ancient pagan customs and have made a pledge about this before God. We will try to obey it. I am asking You to bless me and the others. Ehatii Seion Cockoois N'etty [Your Son] Semeon Kakoish [signed in English]

Interpreted by K. S. Sokolov, Sitka, Alaska, January 23, 1896

[*Library of Congress, Manuscript Division, Alaska Church Collection, D-322*]

Appendix 8

Annual Report of the Condition of the Indian Brotherhood of St. Michael of Sitka (for the Year 1898)

(Excerpts)

There are currently twenty members in the Brotherhood. Two have been expelled for disobeying the statutes. Two have been admitted: a Sitka *toen* Pavel Katliian and his wife Agrippina. This was a very remarkable success for the Brotherhood, since *toen* Katliian is the head of a large Indian clan. The Brotherhood can now hope that its membership will increase and so will its charitable activities, which in the year 1898 consisted of the following: $19.00 was provided by the Brotherhood for the assistance of its members during illness; $20.00 was donated to buy a *darokhranitel'nitsa* [communion vessel] in commemoration of the fiftieth anniversary of the Sitka Cathedral; loans to members were also given from the treasury. Besides financial assistance, Brotherhood members constantly helped each other; provided household help, brought food and fuel for the poor, and were especially considerate to their fellow members when the latter were ill. They also provided some assistance to persons not belonging to the Brotherhood, in accordance with the Christian law of Charity. They tried to follow the statutes of the Brotherhood without transgressions. With the exception of one case, they always abstained from pagan ceremonies, diligently attended the church, listened to the Word of God preached to them there and during their meetings, and tried to live in peace and tranquility. Membership fees were paid fairly regularly. At the present time the treasury contains $54.50.

Chairman of the Sitka Indian Brotherhood of St. Michael, Teacher of the Archbishop Innocent School, Sergei Popov

[*Library of Congress, Manuscript Division, Alaska Church Collection, D-322*]

Appendix 9

A[rchimandrite] A[natolii]
The Frog Case

A Sitka newspaper "Alaskan" reported recently that the famous *xîxch'* or the wooden frog, which two years ago became the cause of a quarrel among Sitka Indians, is once again the center of attention and the reason for unrest. Here is what the newspaper says: "Almost three years ago, during a big potlatch (a ceremony similar to the ancient Slavic memorial feast) given by the Sitka L'uknax̲.ádi in honor of the Taku Indians, the former decided to proclaim the *xîxch'* [frog] their clan emblem. As everybody recalls, at that time Judge Johnson, fearing unrest that could have been caused by the Kiks.ádi who also claim the frog as their clan emblem, left the lawsuit unresolved. He did, however, give the L'uknax̲.ádi a promise that their frog would take its proper place after the court decision is reached.

This was the state of this case until last fall, when Judge Brown turned to it again and announced that the court had no legal right to make any decisions about it. Thus the obstacle against proclaiming the frog a clan emblem had been overcome and soon it was occupying its proper place on the front of a chief's house, despite the protests of the Kiks.ádi.

For a while there were rumors about a mass riot but thanks to an intervention by one official, a written agreement signed by most Indians appeared. It stated that, since they were now Christians and were ruled by civilized people, they wished from now on to do away with all their tribal and religious emblems. But the fact that the warring factions refused to shake hands and destroy their emblems made the agreement of little force.

This was the way things remained for a few days, until Indian policemen heard a rumor that the Kiks.ádi were planning to destroy the infamous frog. To prevent this, they began a careful watch over the three brothers, leaders of the Kiks.ádi, Kukhach, Tuik, and Shkuetl, but there was no real cause for arresting them.

About 3 o'clock, on February 7, the above mentioned brothers accompanied by six of their clan relatives took a specially prepared ladder and made an attack on the frog. Using axes they chopped it up into tiny pieces. Fortunately the *taion* and most of his family inhabiting the houses were away, otherwise there would most likely have been bloodshed there. Having carried out their deed, the brave ones withdrew before the L'uknax̲.ádi had time to assemble and capture them.

Authorities were immediately notified. Five of the attackers, i.e., Kukhach, Tuik, Shkuetl, G. Nishugai, and Tliakutlek, were immediately arrested for riot-

117

ing. Later on, the other four were arrested—Katukish, Tukvan, Kunukis and [?]—and charged with the same crime. All of them were given an opportunity to pay the bail, in order to face a jury trial later on. However, since the bail was high, that is, $1000.00 for each of them, they could not pay such an amount and were put into the Sitka jail.

Whether a stop is finally put to all of this depends primarily on the outcome of the trial. If the instigators are severely punished, it would make a strong impression on the rest of those inclined to riot. In any case, all this unrest involves only the two warring factions and nobody else outside of them should have any reason to worry.

In one of the issues of the *Russian Orthodox American Messenger* for the year 1899, there was an article describing the origins of this famous frog, hence there is no need to repeat it here. Among other things, a comment was made there about the decision of Judge Johnson and the announcement that "the frog should end up in a wood stack to be used as firewood." The article said that, knowing the Indian character, it was difficult to believe that this argument had already been resolved forever.

Nevertheless, when this was written, nobody expected that the affair would become so serious, that nine of the better Sitka Indians would be sitting in jail for chopping up a wooden statue of a frog and would probably subsequently face an even greater punishment for their zeal. The American legal code contains no law against idolatry, but a law forbidding the destruction of an idol has been found. The fact is that the Indians regard the statue of the frog as a kind of deity and the ceremony of raising it to the top of the house as a religious ritual.

However, the present case interests us neither because it raises a question why such ugly phenomena are possible in Sitka, nor because one would like to know whether this trial would end in a severe punishment of the "ringleaders," which would serve as a warning to others not to display statues of all the ancient Indian deities—cohos, seals, ravens, etc. What should concern us, is how to prevent these and other phenomena in the future. Such cases are numerous in the files of the Alaskan court. How many suspected witches have already been killed! How many *nakws'aatí* have been starved to death, drowned in the sea, shot, and so on! Every fall, when the Indians return to their villages from the summer hunting and fishing expeditions, endless "kakhitli" [*kaxéel'*, trouble] or mass quarrels begin, which often end in fights and even murders. Every fall at least five or six witches or *nakws'aatí* are "tied up."

Sooner or later rumors of these crimes reach the authorities and this leads to arrests, trials, and prison sentences. In most cases, the culprit and the defendant is the supposedly bewitched person himself, some sick individual, with paralyzed arms or legs, consumption and so on. There are, however, many unresolved cases of tied-up and murdered *nakws'aatí*. During the examination of these cases in court, it is usually revealed that the tying up of the witch involved a shaman who had been asked by the patient or his relatives to point out the one that had caused the illness.

In short, such investigations reveal that the basis of these crimes are the Indian savagery, superstitions, lack of any comprehension of the law as it is understood by the whites, and the Indian loyalty to their own ancient tribal customs and clan organization. As individual persons most Indians are rather sophisticated fellows. Most of the young people should be considered educated, since they studied in vocational schools or "training schools," as they are called here. But as members of their society, with their tribal notions about kinship, these Indians are the same savages as they were before the encounter with the white man.

All this proves that, while the present enlighteners of Alaska have paid great attention to individual Indians and for that reason have built schools and orphanages for the education of the young generation, nothing has been done to improve the life of the natives in general since the time of the Russian departure from Alaska, [and] the native life has been left intact. Neither the legislation, nor the private initiative of various missionaries and benefactors have touched the family life of the Indians. Indian villages and houses are the same as they were fifty years ago. One would think that the graduates of orphanages and trade schools returning to their villages and families would favorably influence and gradually enlighten their kinsmen. But facts show a very different picture. They have brought home from orphanages and schools only new styles of dress, fashionable haircuts, and many other things which the civilization should turn away from in embarrassment. One does not notice any struggle between the good new ideas and the ancient forces of ignorance and darkness taking place in Indian villages. On the contrary, the new "civilized" generation falls easily under the influence of the old way of life, often adding only destruction and decay to those good qualities that this way of life used to have.

What conclusions can be drawn from all of this? They are both very simple and very significant at the same time. Number one: Sheldon Jackson's system of education of Alaska has totally failed and should finally be replaced by another one, making more sense under the present circumstances. Number two: the native population of Alaska needs special government laws and regulations aimed at the improvement of their public, private, and family life. Until the time when every native is able to understand the duties of an American citizen, until an Indian or an Eskimo is able to sit among white members of the jury and listen to the recommendations made by lawyers and judges, until native villages are able to elect their own representatives to fill various official positions, they must be ruled by local laws.

The exact nature of the reforms that must be introduced, is impossible to describe in a short essay, especially since it is difficult to know all of them. Only an investigation of the affairs on the local level could reveal what must be done and how. Here we would like simply to point out the nature of the reform that could have been beneficial for the natives of Alaska. This reform should primarily affect the issue of the land settlement. The system of alienating large plots of land (reservations) for settling natives, practiced by the United States government, has turned out to be useful only for the creation of misunderstandings and troubles among Indians and whites as well as for causing Indians to die out. It is difficult to accept the theory, whose popularity among the Americans has been increasing, that the Indian is incapable by nature of becoming civilized and that the only good Indian is a dead one. The Alaskan Indian could eventually become as useful a citizen as any emigrant from Europe. But in the meantime he needs special conditions for living. All the Indians should be divided into communities or communes [*obshchestva*] and each community should be given not only the land inhabited by its members but all the places where they catch fish, seals, beavers, etc. These places set aside for their full ownership should be closed to white hunters, and especially large companies whose rapacious methods of hunting have caused trouble for the original local native hunters.

The state would not suffer at all but would only benefit from this. Considering the climate of Alaska, one could predict that, aside from temporary predators, no white hunters would ever live there. In case gold deposits are discovered by an Indian on the communal land or somewhere else, he should enjoy the same privileges as a white miner. If Alaska becomes a state, the Indian should be given the right to leave his commune and become a citizen of the state after passing a certain examination.

Each commune should be headed by *taions* or tribal elders who must be in charge of its affairs. At the present time, the government bestows the title of policeman upon some natives in order to have someone to maintain law and order in Indian villages. While these persons could be useful to the authorities as spies and obliging executors of their will, they usually have no influence among their tribesmen. The crowd knows only its own *taions* who, on their part, constantly try to maintain their prestige and hence openly and secretly oppose every measure originating from the government and implemented by the policemen. At the same time, these *taions* are the strongest defenders of the old ways. This is why various attempts by the government, the mission, or private individuals to eliminate pagan customs and barbarianism among Alaskan natives usually fail, faced with the dark superstitions of the masses. However, if government officials would influence the natives through their *taions*, their efforts would be be opposed, and every measure aimed at improving native social and family life would be quickly accepted and produce positive results.

The essence of the reform, however, must be a change in the existing school system. This change would not simply affect the form but the very spirit and direction of the system. To achieve that one must, first of all, replace the entire party headed by the unsuccessful Sheldon Jackson who has turned out to be unfit for this task. Although, maybe, he could remain in charge of reindeer, if his system of reindeer breeding is successful. The educational system, however, should be turned over to a person of an entirely different spirit. The Indian school should not be separate from the native village, while its teacher must teach not only the alphabet and the spelling of English words, as is done now, but also various trades and crafts relevant to Indian life. In addition the teacher should not only instruct the youngsters but the adults as well. He should be given some power, which would allow him to interfere in the affairs of the commune and to influence its leaders whenever it becomes necessary. To accomplish this is not as difficult as it seems. Alaskan natives are very trusting and like to appeal to priests and teachers for help, as long as the latter wish to spend time with them. The presence in an Indian village of an educated person committed to satisfying native material and spiritual needs would be very beneficial, especially if the Indians knew that this person was authorized by the government. Some form of guardianship over the Indians is absolutely necessary, until they develop an independent civilized life.

An example of the Indian ability to acquire culture and become easily civilized under good supervision and leadership is Metlakatla (Metlakatla of Annette Island, southeastern Alaska). Located on a small island given by the United States government to a tribe of Tsimshian Indians for communal ownership, this village looks like an earthly paradise, compared to other towns. Its inhabitants are hardworking. Under the rule of their elderly pastor W. Duncan, who is also their teacher, *taion*, judge, and the chief member of the council of Indian elders, this village had acquired its own cannery, where last year they prepared 18,000 boxes of canned fish for sale. In addition they have a dock for building boats and their own store with various goods and food supplies. One could predict a bright future for this village. While other native villages are becoming smaller or even disappear every year, Metlakatla will grow and expand.

There are rumors that recently various disorders existing in Alaska have attracted attention of the appropriate officials. Some of the senators, who have visited Alaska as tourists, are seriously considering the necessity of reforms. Among such senators, Gallinger, Perkins, Johns, Foster and others are mentioned.

If they are really interested in doing Alaska some good, they should examine its history and take into consideration the Russian attitude to the natives of Alaska and the measures they undertook to improve the life of these children of nature. Then they would see that half a century ago the Russian colonial genius had already developed a system that brought excellent results in the past and could be useful at present as well. Unfortunately, this system was able to affect only the life of the natives of southwestern Alaska, in the area of Kodiak and the Aleutian Islands, but did not have enough time to become firmly established and to introduce the moral principles of Christian life into its southeastern region.

Otherwise there would not even be a trace of frog cases, shamans, witches and other forms of barbarianism in southeastern Alaska, where, since the departure of the Russians, such phenomena not only did not diminish but seem to have increased.

[*Russian Orthodox American Messenger*, 1901, vol. 5, no. 10, pp. 208-210; no. 11, pp. 233-234.]

Appendix 10

A Letter to the Right Reverend Nikolai, Bishop of the Aleutian Islands and Alaska, from Hieromonk Anatolii of Sitka

January 21 (February 2), 1897

Your Eminence,
My Most Gracious Archpastor:

In one of Your previous letters, Your Grace has expressed a wish that I support my complaints about Presbyterian abuses with facts. In this letter, I hurry to satisfy Your Grace's wish. Without mentioning various previous facts, I consider it my duty to report two most recent incidents that occurred on January 21-23 and January 28 of the current year, 1897.

I. On Thursday, January 21, at 9 o'clock in the morning, an Indian from the Sitka village came to see me and told me that a sick woman, Ekaterina Kakhtutin, the wife of Stephan Katliian, was doing very badly, would die soon, and that her relatives were asking me to come and pray for her. This woman had been ill all winter long. Lately three festering wounds had developed on her neck, and then gangrene of the lungs had supervened. I went and recited the customary prayers over her. She had very little time left. I left her relatives after a consultation, but no more than half an hour later a messenger came back and announced that the woman had died and that her relatives had decided to transfer her body to the house of Ivan Khliantych [L.aanteech], her brother, where one of the sisters of the deceased, Agafiia, was also residing.

The reason for this was the fact that S. Katliian's house was too small and, most importantly, one of the children of the deceased, Aleksander, was also lying in that house, near death. (It is true that he lived only for three days after his mother's funeral.) The relatives asked me to come to the house of I. Khliantych to perform the *litiia* [memorial] service for the deceased. I followed their request and went there about noon, accompanied by the *psalomshchik* [reader] A. Arkhangel'skii. The body of the deceased had already been placed in a coffin and a cover was being finished in the same room. After the *litiia* I was told that, despite the fact that the coffin had already been made and the body had already been placed there, the two oldest sons of Katliian (by his first wife) residing in the Presbyterian mission had ordered another coffin from the mission.

To this I responded that the sons should not oppose their father's will and that the Presbyterian mission had nothing to do with the deceased. Her husband and her own children (there were four of them: Ananii Shikhovat, 19 years old; Mariia Kukanakh, 16; Aleksander L'tutaken, 8; and Aleksandra Kassenka, 5) were all Orthodox, while she herself had been a most zealous Orthodox Christian, and only a few days ago confessed to me and received Holy Communion. Her main wish was that I would bury her properly and would remember her in my prayers. Having said all that, I left them.

Next day, Friday, the 22nd of January, I returned to conduct another *litiia* and found the deceased lying in two coffins! The one in which she had been placed yesterday was now put inside another one, whose lid stood there too, with an inscription "in her name." "What does this mean?" I asked them. They replied that the Presbyterian sons had come and done it, saying that such were the orders of government officials. "And what does the husband, Katliian, think about this?" I inquired. They replied that at first he resisted, but finally decided that until the funeral things could remain the way they were. Having performed the *litiia* and listened to those explanations, I left them full of indignation against the Presbyterian tricks. Little did I know that their impudence would go even further.

An hour or so later I went to the Indian school. A few minutes after I had come there, the eldest son of the deceased, Ananii, arrived to tell me that his mother was being carried away by the Presbyterians. Not understanding what was happening I told Arkhangel'skii who happened to be with me: "Let us go and see what is happening there."

And so we went. As soon as we passed the house of Iantan, we saw the following picture. Two Indian policemen, Bean and Jackson (Anaxóots), with two other fellows unknown to me, and under the direction of the minister A.E. Austin and the assistant teacher of the Indian public school, Mrs. Campbell, were dragging the coffin. The were followed by Governor James Sheakley, Marshal [W. Z.?] Williams, the government interpreter S. I. Kostromitinov, several employees of the Presbyterian mission, and behind them a huge crowd of Indians stretching along the entire village and filling the air with crying, howling, and wild lamentations. The minute we appeared on the scene, they began to haul the coffin hurriedly up to the high porch of the house of Taviat. I let Mr. Austin with the coffin pass me, but having found myself face to face with the officials, I could not refrain from asking them what it all meant. The Governor replied that they were just about to go to my house and give explanations. Marshal Williams began immediately to explain that this was done following a complaint of Mr. Austin who had been asked to interfere by the children of the deceased. They told him that Khliantych was trying to rob them and that he had transferred the body to his house under the pretense of making the coffin but with real intention to seize her property.

I was deeply outraged by this lying and juggling of the facts. Little as I know about American laws, I have a good idea, nevertheless, of the duties of the marshal and the governor; I understand very well that property issues are not within their jurisdiction but only within that of the court. In this case there was also a patent distortion of facts. Therefore I tried, as far as circumstances permitted, to explain to the Marshal that there were no solid reasons to accuse Kliantych of some criminal intentions. He had taken the body of the deceased with the consent and desire of her husband and her own children. Besides the husband, Khliantych was her closest relative—her true blood brother. Generally it is difficult to determine kinship relationships among the Indians, since none of them marry according to the manner of white people but live according to their own customs. As far as the two petitioners, the two oldest sons of Katliian, are concerned, they were not related to her in any way and were acting against their father's will.

"In view of all these facts," I announced, "I find your orders incorrect, Mr. Marshal. And since you have taken the liberty without my permission to dispose of my priestly regalia and articles pertaining to the divine service of the Orthodox Church, which have been placed on and near the coffin, such as a stole, a censer, an icon of Our Savior, a candlestick, and the pall, I consider your actions to be disrespectful of Orthodoxy, amounting almost to violence against it." My last words addressed to the Marshal and the Governor were the following: "In the name of the law, I protest against the actions that have taken place here and find it impossible to perform my duties with regard to the funeral."

Half an hour later, when the excitement had abated somewhat, I went to the Governor's office accompanied by A.M. Arkhangel'skii and S.I. Kostromitinov. The Governor received us and a rather lengthy conversation took place. I tried to prove to the Governor that his and the Marshal's orders were illegal. It turned out that the Governor did not even know whether the two Presbyterians who had ordered a coffin from the mission were the deceased woman's relatives or not, and whether they were living in their father's house or not . . . . He also did not know why they had placed the body of the deceased in the house of Taviat. When I explained to him that these were not her own children but her stepsons, that they were acting against the will of their father with whom they had not lived for a long time, that the house of Taviat was not inhabited by any relatives of the deceased, and that the body of the dead woman had been taken there upon Mr. Austin's instruction because it was used for Presbyterian prayer meetings, the Governor agreed, saying all of that had been done by the Marshal and not him, and that he would agree to everything we ask for, if the Marshal would have no objections. Therefore he suggested that we speak to the Marshal again.

And so we went to the Marshal's office. I asked him directly whether he would allow the coffin to be taken back to the house of the husband of the deceased. He replied that he would agree to that but would never agree to have the body of the deceased to return to Khliantych's house. When I asked him why, he responded that Khliantych wanted to take the property of the deceased. "But Khliantych has not said that," I objected, "and since he has not said that and has not done anything, he should not be treated as a robber." "Although

Khliantych has not said that he would take the property, he is a bad man and would certainly do so," replied the Marshal. "Maybe he is a bad man in other cases, and I do not intend to defend him. But in this case, I believe he is right, since he is the closest relative of the deceased and has taken the body at the request of her husband and children," I replied. Then the Marshal, in his turn, referred to the Governor, saying that the latter had invited him to interfere in the affair. Responding to that, Kostromitinov told him that the Governor himself had referred us to him.

Having heard that, the Marshal asked us to accompany him to the Governor's office. Following us, Mrs. Campbell accompanied by one of the Presbyterian sons entered the office. A general discussion began, in the course of which the Governor and the Marshal found out for the first time that the deceased whose body they had been carrying was lying in an Orthodox coffin and not a Presbyterian one. More correctly she was now lying in two coffins, since the mission coffin, being larger and made later, served only as a container for the Orthodox one. All of this was confirmed by Mrs. Campbell. It was amusing to see how indignant the two officials became. Their indignation knew no bounds. The Marshal ordered Mrs. Campbell to transfer the body of the deceased from the Orthodox coffin to the Presbyterian one immediately and then walked out slamming the door. The Governor confirmed the order of his colleague.

Once again I had to protest, though in vain, and to make them understand that the new order would be another obstacle in my carrying out of the priestly duties pertaining to the funeral. Just as earlier it was improper for me to conduct the service in a missionary house, so now it was even more improper to perform it with a missionary coffin decorated with heretical emblems, that it would be for me the same as conducting the service dressed as a Buddhist bonze. I explained that Orthodox Christians have their own funeral rituals and make their own inscriptions and emblems on coffins of their deceased. In conclusion I added that if the Governor and the Marshal did not want to have the body of the deceased buried in the coffin made by her husband and other Orthodox relatives, they should allow me to build a third coffin at the expense of my church which had the means to do it. But this proposition was rejected as well.

In the course of the discussion, the officials did not spare me many caustic remarks; the Governor told me directly that I, a foreigner and a newcomer, was teaching them rather than the other way around, and that, if I did not like American laws, I could leave Sitka, and so on. To these and other similar remarks I replied that I was not trying to teach them and was not trying to oppose American laws. On the contrary, I was trying to have these laws followed properly and that it was not I who started the whole trouble. I said that until I met the known procession in the Indian village, I had no intention to visit their offices, despite the fact that Orthodoxy had already been insulted by the presence of the Presbyterian coffin. I added that we, the Orthodox people, have already gotten used to such tricks and do not drag Presbyterians to offices, but when authorities interfered, the affair assumed an official significance, since the government representatives themselves were violating the freedom of worship. I told them that I had come to them not as a foreigner but as a representative of the local Orthodox Church, among whose members were American citizens, and that I was defending their rights rather than my own personal ones.

While I went home after that conversation, deeply saddened by the outcome of the affair, Mrs. Campbell hurried immediately to transfer the body of the deceased from the Orthodox into the Presbyterian coffin. That operation was accomplished successfully. All that was more than I could stand. And so I made a new attempt to bring the Governor to his senses by sending him the following note:

— —

Sitka, Alaska
January 22, 1897

The Honorable James Sheakley,
Governor of Alaska

Dear Sir:

If I am not authorized and permitted by you to bury the deceased Indian woman, who died yesterday, in the coffin made according to the customs of the Greek Orthodox Church, I would be compelled to refuse to bury her.

The Russian Church has sufficient means to make a coffin required by its laws.

Very respectfully yours,
Rev. Hieromonk Anatolii Kamenskii
Priest of the Orthodox Church
of Sitka

— —

About half an hour later I saw from the window of my apartment a hearse with a pair of horses being driven fast from the Presbyterian Mission to the Kolosh village, with Mr. Austin running behind it. A thought crossed my mind that this respectable Presbyterian minister was running so fast not to perform a good deed but to bury the body of the poor Indian woman. I decided to go and see what else the minister and the officials were going to do. Along the way I picked up Arkhangel'skii and both of us went there slowly. We found the hearse standing near the public Indian school surrounded by a crowd of Indians. I asked them where the body was and learned that it was still at the house where the Governor and the Marshal had put it, and had not been moved to her husband's house. "What did the hearse come for?" I asked. "To take the body," they replied, "although she was an Orthodox, Mr. Austin is going to bury her in his cemetery, where a grave has already been prepared yesterday." The last piece of information puzzled me somewhat, suggesting that the outcome of this affair had been expected for quite some time.

At that moment, two Indian policemen, Bean and Jackson, came up to me along with the interpreter of Judge Rogers, an Indian named Peter Church, and told me that they had just returned from the judge who had told them to inform Katliian, the husband of the deceased, to ignore any interference or threats, and to take the body of his wife and bury it from the house that he himself would choose and to use any coffin he liked, even a cracker box. The policemen were on their way to carry out the judge's order.

The last phrase of the judge was evidently aimed at me. Nevertheless, Judge Rogers' interference did bring positive results. Afterward I was told that soon after the Governor had received my note, the Judge met with him and had severely reprimanded both him and the Marshal. Having spoken with the policemen, I now understood why the hearse had been kept waiting. Having found out that the husband of the deceased was at the Governor's office, I immediately went there. As I entered the office, I saw the following picture.

In the middle of the room stood the grey-haired old man S. Katliian, speaking to those present. Nearby stood his older children—a son and a daughter—with their heads bent down. At the door was a large crowd of Indians and a few Americans. Closer to the table sat Rev. A.E. Austin, the Governor, the Marshal, the government interpreter, and others. The Indian Peter Church acted as an interpreter. The old man spoke with great fervor. Periodically he would address Mr. Austin. I did not understand Katliian's speech. At one point Austin tried to respond to the old man. Taking advantage of that interruption, I asked to have Katliian's speech translated for me. The entire content of the speech was related to me only afterwards. The old man said something like this:

"I have lived a long life, but never experienced such a trouble. Two days ago my wife died and for two days I have not had a single piece of bread. Her death brought terrible sadness to me but this trouble is even worse. And all of this is your fault," said the old man, turning to Austin. "Both of us are grey-haired men now; imagine if your wife died and your children would act against your will—how would you like that?" Mr. Austin tried to respond, saying that his children had appealed to him on Katliian's behalf. But the old man vehemently denied that, saying that the missionary had believed them without investigating the matter . . . . Further on Katliian asked that an end should be put to the trouble and said that his only wish was to be allowed to bury his wife according to the Orthodox rite. He finished by saying: "This was her own wish, and also such is the wish of her children and myself."

I added to the old man's speech that they were all witnessing something unheard of, which could not be endured without being greatly moved. "I cannot look at this bent old man without compassion. And as a local representative of the Russian Church, I was deeply disturbed by this affair. Who would ever imagine that, without any reason, the body of a Christian woman who had died peacefully would be treated like that of an animal, all but dragged by the feet along the street, without any regard for the lamentations and cries of her relatives, to whom this body is so dear. In addition the body is being transferred from one coffin into another at the whim of strangers trying to achieve certain goals . . . .

Are these the methods of the Presbyterian propaganda, which advertises itself and its deeds so loudly here, while humiliating the followers of their creeds all the time? Is physical and moral violence their substitute for the peaceful propagation of the Gospel? And all this in a land of freedom where the law treats all denominations equally!"

My speech was interrupted by Mr. Austin who replied that neither Presbyterians nor he personally have anything to do with all this. "I would like to believe this, Mr. Austin," I replied, "but all the facts contradict your words; how can you explain, for example, your presence at the head of that shameful procession that I have met today in the Indian village?" To my question Austin replied that he had been invited.

Our conversation was interrupted by the Governor who began to attack me with great irritation, saying that I was the cause of the entire trouble, that I was inciting the people, that he considered me a "bad" and an "imprudent" man, and, since I had come to America, I should know how to behave myself, and that it would be better if I left Sitka.

To his speech I had to respond that he had no reasons or rights to insult me like that, without first pointing out of what my ignorance and disrespect to American laws consisted. I added that I had never said a single disrespectful word about American laws nor had ever broken them, on the contrary, at the moment, I was trying to make everybody follow those laws.

"Do you intend to bury the woman," the governor asked me. I replied, "I know Judge Rogers' decision about this matter and have no objections against the instructions he has given to the policemen. Only let the husband make his own arrangements." The Marshal interfered and asked in which coffin and from which house I was planning to bury her. "I shall do whatever the husband says," was my reply. "After all that has happened today, I do not have the courage to continue these difficulties. Ask the husband."

The Marshal replied that he still held to his opinion that the body should not be taken to the house of Khliantych. I promised to make a concession on this point and even to influence my parishioners in that direction. As for the other questions, I requested to consult with the husband once more and find out his opinion.

Katliian was told what was expected of him. He stood up and replied that all he wanted was the end of this disturbance, that the body of the deceased be brought to his house, where she had died and had been placed in a coffin made by him and her other Orthodox relatives, and that she be buried according to the rites of the Orthodox Church. As far as the other coffin, in order not to offend anybody, he wished to have it placed inside the grave, letting the deceased rest in two coffins.

After that the Governor asked me once again whether I intended to conduct the funeral and I replied "yes."

Next day, at 10 o'clock in the morning, an extraordinary procession was moving along the streets of Sitka. Women were carrying the body of the deceased to the Russian Orthodox church in two coffins, with two covers being carried in front of them. All the faces reflected if not joy then at least satisfaction that the body of the poor woman was finally going to find rest in the ground, although desecrated by heretics.

I bring this instance of the abuse of the Orthodox in Sitka to the attention of Your Grace, hoping that it would attract attention. The entire incident has been witnessed besides myself by the *psalomshchik* Arkhangel'skii who testifies to the truth of everything written here by affixing his own signature hereto.

Your Grace's
Most Humble Servants
Hieromonk Anatolii
Psalomshchik Aleksandr Arkhangel'skii

————————————————————————————————————

II. Another incident involved the children of the same old man Katliian and took place on January 28. His eldest daughter, Mariia Kukanakh came to see me and told me that the assistant teacher of the Indian public school, Mrs. Campbell, accompanied by one of their Presbyterian brothers, has just arrived at their house and wants to take them to the Presbyterian mission, that is, herself and her older brother (the younger one had just died). This time I happened to have the interpreter, Kharlampii Sokolov, with me. And so both of us went to Katliian's house to find out what had happened.

The old man told the same story, adding only that Mrs. Campbell told them that she had come following the Governor's order; it was supposedly the Governor who was ordering the children to be taken to the Presbyterian mission.

Without thinking twice I asked the old man to get dressed and together with his older children to accompany us to Judge Rogers. Before we had reached the court, we met the Judge and Mr. Kostromitinov coming toward us. Katliian immediately made his complaint through Kostromitinov. The Judge listened and said that no one had any more right to take a man's children away than to take his head. Therefore he could not believe that there was any truth in Mrs. Campbell's assertion and advised us to go to the Governor and find out the truth.

All of us, with the exception of the Judge, proceeded to the Governor's office. He listened to us and positively denied having given any such order to Mrs. Campbell. This settled the issue.

The fact that Mrs. Campbell did make the assertion about the Governor's alleged order is testified to by many Indians who were present there.

While reporting this additional fact to Your Eminence, My Most Gracious Archpastor, I have the honor of being Your Eminence's most obedient servant.

Hieromonk Anatolii
Sitka
January 21 (February 2), 1897

[*Russian Orthodox American Messenger*, vol. 1, no. 12, 1897, pp. 227-239.]

Appendix 11

A PETITION
TO HIS EXCELLENCY MR. KOTZEBUE
IMPERIAL RUSSIAN AMBASSADOR TO
WASHINGTON

Your Excellency:

All of us, the undersigned Orthodox residents of Sitka, both of Russian and Native descent, take the liberty of addressing you with an entreaty that you extend your protection to the Russian Orthodox Church in Alaska and defend it against oppression and violence of all kinds, which it suffers at the hand of the Presbyterian missionaries and other persons, and not infrequently even at those of government officials belonging to the Presbyterian Church.

The Orthodox natives, Indians, numbering no less than 482, are continually subjected to abuses of every kind. They cannot find protection in the courts and other official places dominated by Presbyterians.

There are rather frequent cases when government officials, members of the Presbyterian Church, violate the rights of the Orthodox people by personal interference. Such a case occurred on January 22 of the current year, 1897, when with the personal participation of Governor J. Sheakley and Marshal Williams, violence was done to an Orthodox Indian *taion* (chief) Katliian. He was forced to bury his wife in two coffins, while the rector of the Orthodox church, who protested the interference of government officials in this purely ecclesiastical matter, was called a "bad man" by the Governor, who used other insulting words as well. This case will probably be immediately reported to Your Excellency by His Eminence, the Right Reverend Nikolai, Bishop of Alaska and the Aleutian Islands.

Every year news of similar or even worse insults of Russian clergymen are received from remote corners of Alaska. In the near future Sitka is expecting a new Governor, a Presbyterian pastor J.G. Brady, while the position of the Marshal will be occupied by W.A. Kelly, the former superintendent of the Presbyterian Mission. This is expected to result in even greater persecution of Orthodoxy.

In view of all this we take the liberty to petition Your Excellency:

1) To appeal to the Government in Washington and to report this condition of Orthodoxy in Alaska, asking it to impress upon its officials sent to Alaska the duty of paying the closest attention to the abuses committed by the Presbyterian Mission and to be impartial to Orthodoxy, in strict adherence to the treaty made between Russia and the United States in the year 1867, and particularly

not to allow themselves to persecute members of the Orthodox Church, in order to avoid possible unrest.

2) To appeal most humbly to His Imperial Majesty, the Emperor Nikolai Aleksandrovich, Autocrat of All Russia, to appoint a Representative of the Russian Imperial Government, with a right to reside in Sitka, to whom the Russian subjects residing here as well as all the Orthodox inhabitants of Alaska could appeal in cases of persecution of their faith and not infrequent cases of violation of other provisions of the above mentioned treaty, besides [provision] number 3. Whereto we affix our signatures: [Over 70 signatures of Russian and Creoles follow, some in Russian and some in English.]

[*Russian Orthodox American Messenger*, vol. 1, no. 12, 1897, pp. 240-242]

[*Translator's Commentary*: this petition appeared in the *Russian Orthodox American Messenger* in English and Russian. I have slightly edited the English version to bring it closer to the Russian original.]

Appendix 12

A PETITION
TO THE PRESIDENT OF THE UNITED
STATES

Dear Sir:

From the very time when the United States raised its flag here and throughout the entire Territory, our people have not ceased to appeal directly to the Government in Washington through its representatives, the most prominent chiefs and leaders. We have done this, despite our knowledge of the presence of Government representatives here, such as the Governor and other officials. The reason for this is the following: our just and legal demands cannot find satisfaction here. We know that the Russian government at the time of the transfer of Alaska to the United States did not sell us as slaves but obtained certain rights and privileges for us, which were subsequently approved and legalized by the Congress.

Section 8 of the Organic Act, which provides the civil government for Alaska, says that neither the Indians nor other persons inhabiting this territory shall be disturbed in the possession of any lands actually in their use, occupancy, or claimed by them. On the strength of this law, we always understood that every Indian has a right to dispose of his own life and property, whether personal possessions or real estate, such as lands, forests, lagoons, some small bays and rivers where we could procure food for ourselves and other necessities of existence.

We always thought that the civil government sent here by Washington should punish criminals, whether white or native, so that if a white man spills the blood of an Indian or, on the contrary, an Indian spills the blood of a white man, justice would punish them equally. But in reality such equality never existed. It is true that the first four years of our life under the protection of the American Eagle remain in our memory as a period of pure peace, without any cloud of misunderstanding between a white man and an Indian. It is also true that from the time of Governor Kinkead till that of Governor Swineford, when the scales of justice were in the hands of Mr. Haskett, we could still sometimes obtain satisfaction of our demands, but in the remaining time there was no justice at all. It does not exist right now either. It has perished.

In our mind's eye rise the images of our 28 friends and relatives who perished innocently at the hands of white people. Of course, we always complained to United States courts, but in all the courts we received only promises but never any satisfaction. Not a single white murderer, ending with the last one, named

Mills, who had killed a native, Donald Austin, received an appropriate punishment and still enjoys total freedom.

Despite all this, we never lost faith in the Government in Washington, but were only forced to lose faith in the persons sent here by the Government.

From the Government we have always expected and are still expecting to receive satisfaction of our lawful demands. We believe that the promises made by the Vice President, who has recently visited Sitka, were not empty words. And at the present time, remembering the promises made by a member of the Government Commission, Geo. R. Tingle, to try once more to help us, we still hope that our petition will reach the desired end. Without mentioning our previous petitions made during the last few years we appeal only about the issues listed here:

1) Not to allow Mr. Brady to pass through the middle of our village, along the narrow beach between the water and our houses where we keep our canoes and other things. In addition, to forbid him to destroy buildings and other property in the process of construction of the road. We do not lay claims on the land which he now owns, despite the fact that it had been the property of our ancestors since time immemorial and was used by them as a cemetery. It is enough that he illegally took possession of that land and used some of the bones to bank his road, while he threw others in the water. We do not wish these works to go on and do not wish other white people to follow Mr. Brady's example.

2) We ask that Mr. Smith, the superintendent of the Baranoff Packing Company, would be forbidden to take away our lagoons, bays and streams where we used to fish long before the arrival of white people. We wish that he would do the necessary fishing only with our consent. We demand that he stops throwing pieces of wood and tree trunks across the streams to prevent fish from going there to spawn. His fishing methods in the last eight years have made such places as Redoubt Bay, Cross Sound, Hoonah, Whale Bay, Necker Bay, and Redfish Bay virtually empty.

3) We do not want American saloons. We ask the Government to close them down. Tramps and idle people such as soldiers and sailors, bring whiskey into our midst from those establishments, they make our wives and daughters drunk and often seduce them in that state. We have brought such cases to the attention of local authorities, but always with the same result: the white man remained unpunished, while the native was forced to pay fines, go to jail, and so forth. Saloons and other places of amusement are not needed for the wellbeing of our daughters. We do not want a civilization that not only does not close such establishments but even encourages them. We do not want education that tears our daughters away from their homes and alienates them, teaching them the English language, which only makes it easier and more profitable for them to engage in prostitution. Drinking has brought adultery into our families, and

adultery has torn apart our family bonds. We do not want to look at this terrible evil with indifference, but want to have such crimes punished not by light fines, but in a way that some real good would result. We do not see the necessity to populate saloons and dance halls in Sitka and Juneau with our educated daughters.

We could have gone on and on with this petition. We have uncovered the facts and ask the Government to pay at least some attention to us. We never received answers to our previous petitions, maybe because of the fault of the mediator who had promised to deliver them. Consequently we now ask the Government to address the reply to Khliantych, the head chief of the Sitka tribe. We have the honor to sign this petition as Your most humble servants.

John Khliantych
Tom Katzekoni
Sergei Anlizhe
Aleksandr Natzlen
Pavel Katliian
Oushkinakk
Nowaya
Saha
Vattan
Quitka

[*Russian Orthodox American Messenger*, vol. 1, no. 12, 1897, pp. 242-246]

[*Translator's Commentary*: this petition was printed in the *Russian Orthodox American Messenger* in English and Russian. I have slightly edited the English version to bring it closer to the Russian original. The spelling of the names of the native leaders who signed the petition follows the original.]

Appendix 13

Excerpts from a Report [on the State of the Sitka Parish in 1896] *to the Right Reverend Nikolai, Bishop of the Aleutian Islands and Alaska, from Hieromonk Anatolii, Dean of Clergy of the Sitka District, February 5, 1897*

In addition to providing instruction in the dogma of Orthodoxy and the rules of Christian piety and devotion, the work of the Indian mission involved a struggle against the ancient forms of their social life contradicting Christian morality, and pagan customs. The Indians still adhere strongly to their tribal way of life. There are several clans in Sitka, the major ones among them are: the Kaagwaantaan, the Kiks.ádi and the L'uknax.ádi. According to their ancient customs, men of one tribe [moiety] always marry women of the other, e.g., Kaagwaantaan men marry Kiks.ádi women, L'uknax.ádi men marry Kaagwaantaan women, and vice versa. Children of these marriages receive their names not from their father, as it is done among all the tribes of the white race, but from their mothers. If a mother is Kaagwaantaan, so are her children.

If one of the parents dies, the entire property of the deceased goes not to the children and the surviving parent, but to the [matrilineal] relatives of the deceased. Because of this, the Indians are strongly opposed to legalized marriages, since the latter could become an obstacle to this form of inheritance and other tribal customs. The first opportunity available to the [matrilineal] relatives of the deceased to become involved in the property affairs is the funeral conducted and paid for by them collectively. They provide the coffin, invite the coffin-makers [*grobovshchiki*], the pall-bearers [*nosil'shchiki*], and the criers [*plakal'shchiki*], who always belong to the opposite tribe [moiety] and are paid rather generously, especially if a large inheritance is expected to be received from the estate of the deceased.

This tribal way of life is the foundation of other old pagan customs: *amanatstvo* [hostage exchange], memorial feasts and dances, dances accompanying the construction [dedication] of a new *barabora*, etc.

All this evil became the target of both the Church and private propaganda. The Indian Society of Temperance and Mutual Aid, whose major goal is the elimination of this very evil, had to endure a difficult test. Twice things came to a trial, when members of the society had to defend their right to bury their fellow members at their own expense and without pagan rituals.

By the beginning of 1897, the Society's membership should have been forty-one, but last fall, when a most lively season of pagan memorial feasts [*trizny*] began in Sitka, a number of people were expelled from the Society for failing to fulfill the promises made under oath . . . . In addition several members passed away, so that, as of January 1, 1897, twenty-four members remained in the

Society.

At the present time Society members possess and wear badges similar to those worn by members of the Sitka Creole Brotherhood. They are gathering strength to purchase an icon of the Holy Archstratig Mikhail, patron saint of the Society, as well as a gonfalon [khorugv'].

The brotherhood treasury is in order, which cannot always be expected from the Indians. The Society's safe with the money is kept in the cathedral's storage room.

In addition to the dark forces of paganism, we had to fight against another evil enemy of Orthodoxy, which in Sitka is the Presbyterian Mission under the leadership of Pastor Austin. It used every opportunity to oppose Orthodoxy. All kinds of excuses were invented in order to interfere in Orthodox affairs. Sometimes the Presbyterian Mission rallied around the flag of American patriotism and found Orthodoxy to be the enemy of the American freedom; sometimes it claimed that Orthodoxy was ignorant and crude and then attacked it in the name of the ideals of enlightenment. Not infrequently it joined forces with paganism, simply to use any available opportunity to act against its enemy. Never before and nowhere else has the Jesuit principle "the aim justifies the means" found such a shameful application as in the activity of Austin and Co. Not to mention the propaganda that had a certain aura of legality and enjoyed some support from the local officials, members of the Presbyterian Church.

The public school for Indian children has been turned into a hall for the evening meetings of Presbyterian Indians. Since the beginning of the school year 1896/97, Miss Campbell, an Indian woman living in the Mission, has been made a teacher's assistant. In order to procure a place for her in the public school they had to lie: the number of students attending that school was changed from 43 to 143. Miss Campbell's shameless propaganda in the school and in the Indian village is outrageous.

Despite these desperate efforts of the Presbyterians to oppose Orthodoxy, during 1896 sixty-five persons joined our Church in Sitka: forty-eight from paganism, fourteen from Presbyterianism, two from Catholicism and one from Judaism . . . .

> Your Grace's
> Most Humble Servant
> The Dean of Clergy
> of the Sitka District
> Hieromonk Anatolii

February 5, 1897
[Library of Congress, Manuscript Division, Alaska Church Collection, D-432]

Appendix 14

Information on the Condition of the St. Michael Cathedral of Sitka for the Year 1897. (Written to Bishop Nikolai of the Aleutian Islands and Alaska by Archimandrite Anatolii.)

[Excerpts]

An attempt has been made to organize a parish trusteeship. For the last ten years, the church *starosta* has not been elected by the parish but appointed upon the recommendation of the clergy by the diocese authorities. Consequently none of the parish members are informed about or involved in the process of conducting the practical affairs of the church. This situation has led some evil tongues to saying unpleasant things about the clergy and the *starosta*. On the other hand, such an indifferent attitude of parish members to their church results unfavorably on the church finances . . . .

It was decided that the best solution to this problem would be the establishment of a parish trusteeship, consisting not only of the Russians and Creoles but of the Indians as well, so that the trustees could serve as intermediaries between the clergy and the *starosta*, on the one hand, and the parish, on the other. The joint meeting of all the parishioners elected, and Your Grace confirmed, the following trustees: three Creoles, Il'ia Bol'shanin, Vasilii Shergin, and Vasilii Kashevarov, and two Indians, Ioann Khliantych and Pavel Katliian. Their duties included, among other things, witnessing the monthly accounting of the church money, in addition they were given certain rights to take part in charitable efforts to help the poorest parish members with the available church resources. All of this corresponded quite well to the local need.

However, for a while the new institution could not establish itself firmly. Its initial efforts met an unfavorable reception from the *starosta*, who threatened to resign if the trustees were allowed to take any part in the practical affairs of the church. This has placed the trustees in a most uncertain situation. Only the future will show the outcome of this confrontation of the two forces within the parish . . . .

In the Indian Society of Temperance, the chairmanship of the teacher S. Popov is not bringing any real benefits. Nothing can be done there without the parish priest. The Indians consider only his word to be authoritative. Consequently, the parish priest should be the chairman of that society. It is not easy for anybody to admit his mistakes, but in this case, where the good of Orthodoxy is involved, I must admit having made two big mistakes, when I resigned from being the chairman of the Russian Brotherhood and the Indian Society.

My punishment was that as an ex-chairman I had to do twice as much as a chairman.

Since the tremendous importance of the school, especially a church school, in the life of the parish has been recognized, serious attention was paid to improving the local educational system. The orphanage school, which in the past academic year has been renamed Archbishop Innocent's School [uchilishche] now gives the opportunity to the young male population to be educated and brought up in a spirit of Russian Orthodoxy. During the five years of its existence, the school has educated a whole generation of Russians and Creoles . . . .

In our efforts to educate the parish members, we did not forget those who need education most, i.e., the Indians. Until now there was no special school for them. Although Indian children were educated separately from white ones, classes for them were conducted in one of the vacant church-owned houses in the port, far from the Indian village. At the present time this inconvenience has been eliminated. A new building for the Indian school has been erected at the Trinity cemetery. As far as its location and construction, this is the best of all private and government schools in Sitka. The building is also designed for the evening meetings of adult Indians, during which they are taught the basics of Orthodoxy by the clergy.

The school was solemnly dedicated on the 8th/20th of March, at 2 p.m., with a very large group of Indians and Russians present . . . . Following the dedication, a conversation [beseda] was conducted with the Indians, and at 7 p.m. pictures from the Bible were shown with the help of a magic lantern . . . . The success of the Orthodox Indian mission in Sitka is clearly demonstrated by the fact that during the year 1897, 62 persons have joined the Church.

Having the honor of relating this information to Your Grace, I remain

Your Grace's
Most Humble Servant
Archimandrite Anatolii

[Library of Congress, Manuscript Division, Alaska Church Collection, D-322]

Appendix 15

Christmas-tide in Sitka

January 7, 1898
Sitka, Alaska

Celebrations of the Nativity in Sitka began with the American Christmas. On the eve of that day a Christmas party [*elka*, lit. "Christmas-tree party"] for the children was organized in the court room; the money for the event was raised by the town residents. This children's festivity was a kind of examination for them. In the presence of their parents, they had to demonstrate their achievements in the study of their native language [Russian] and singing. Children of Indians were not forgotten either. On December 24 (new style) at 3 p.m., the Christmas party at the court room was attended by the students of the Russian Orthodox Indian school together with their teacher, psalm-reader Arkhangel'skii. The children were invited by the master of ceremonies of the event, Mrs. Johnson, the wife of Alaska's Chief Judge. About 3 p.m. I visited the Indian school where the children had gathered waiting to go to the Christmas party. There were about 20 boys and girls in the classroom. The boys were wearing short jackets and trousers, and the girls—light-colored dresses. Despite the winter season, some were wearing straw hats. Only their dark-tanned faces reminded one that they were Indian children . . . . Some of them had books in their hands, which turned out to be Russian primers and prayer books in the Indian [Tlingit] language. I approached one of the boys and using signs asked him to read the primer. He opened the book and fluently and correctly pronounced several Russian phrases. Some of the children recited several prayers in Russian and Indian [Tlingit] from memory.

At 3 o'clock the children came to the court room. They had never seen anything like that in their own dirty houses. There the only entertainment they had were the dances and wild songs of their parents, telling them about their terrifying past. Here among the white people, they are surrounded with attention and love; they are entertained with games, songs, etc. Having received their Christmas presents, the children went home. The main celebration took place in the evening. By 7 o'clock children from all of the schools—public, Presbyterian mission, Russian parochial school for girls, and the Russian orphanage—began to gather. The children sat in the front, the whites—Americans and Russians—behind them.

The children's festivity began. One after another, each boy and girl came out and read their English poems. It seemed that each student and each school tried to excel the others. The children of our Russian orphanage delighted everybody

141

with their skillful reading. Here the Americans could see how their own native language was studied in the Russian schools. Between the reading the children sang American songs. Our children sang American songs on their own to the great delight of the audience. At the end of the program our children sang the Russian national anthem "God Save the Tsar!," accompanied on the piano by Mrs. Johnson, who prepared the children for this party. Everybody liked our anthem because of its majestic harmony. In the end the children were given presents.

A special Christmas party was organized for the Indian children at the Russian orphanage during the first day of the Russian Christmas (Nativity). At 8 p.m. the orphanage's classroom was filled with Indians and their children. A Christmas tree stood in the corner. The children sat in the front on benches, boys on the one side and girls on the other; a large group of adult Indians sat behind them.

"Our Christmas party," they kept saying to each other; one could see on their faces how happy they were when their children came out to the center of the room to read "speeches" in Russian and their own language, and to sing about the Russian Tsar "Ýak'éi, tlax̱ ɣak'éi, Anooshi aankáawu" ("Glory, glory to our Russian Tsar . . . "). The orphanage students sang several Russian songs and the Russian national anthem for them. Each Indian child received a present. At 9 p.m., the Indians and their children started to go home.

On the second day of the Russian Christmas (Nativity), another Christmas party took place at the Russian orphanage. The orphanage children learned several Russian and English poems and songs. The "Russian Christmas party" was attended by all of the Russian and American inhabitants of Sitka. All the government officials received invitation cards. The arrival of the guests began at 7 p.m. All of the officials were present: Alaska's Governor J.G. Brady and Mrs. Brady, U.S. Judge C.S. Johnson and Mrs. Johnson, U.S. Attorney Burton E. Bennet and Mrs. Bennet, and others. The corridors adjacent to the classroom were filled with people. The room was decorated with the Russian and American flags; portraits of His Majesty, Her Majesty, the President of the United States, and the Right Reverend Nikolai, Bishop of Alaska and the Aleutians, were decorated with greens and flowers. The evening began with the students of the [Archbishop] Innocent school and the female students of the parish school singing the Russian anthem accompanied by the organ. After that the children took turns reading poems in Russian and English. Between the reading of poems, Russian and American songs were sung. The orderly behavior of the children as well as their reading and singing delighted the public, which applauded after each performance. Americans were amazed that the children could easily read in two languages, despite the fact that some of them had not spent even two years in the orphanage. Governor J.G. Brady announced that he was amazed by the children's achievements and talents.

The evening ended with the singing of the American anthem "My Country" and a Russian one, "Our Lord is Glorified in Zion." All the children without exception received presents and went to bed. All of the officials and other guests were invited by Fr. Archimandrite Anatolii to his residence. The guest hall was filled with visitors, including all of the officials (with the Governor among them) and other Americans who had attended the Christmas party. The guests were offered tea, chocolate, and fruit. Here, in the hall, they exchanged their opinions, inquired about the life of the children, their education and upbringing, etc. At 10 p.m., all the guests left after thanking the Russians for their hospitality and the party. The adult members of the Russian church—Russians and Indians—will also remember this past Christmas-tide in Sitka.

Among the Indians, there still exists a custom of celebrating their former heathen fests with heathen rituals. During these rituals, all the participants change from European clothes into their old traditional ones—animal skins, feathers, with weapons and scalps. Having gathered together, they dance, shake their weapons, sing wild songs about the bloody glorious events of the past, appeal to spirits, tear up blankets and give out pieces as payments for payments for mutual injuries and insults, distribute gifts, etc. Following Archimandrite Anatolii's suggestion some of the Indians organized a society for fighting against heathen rituals and superstitions. One of the first goals of this society was to eliminate heathen rituals among its own members, and this was in fact accomplished. Contrary to Indian customs, members of the Society will their property to their own children and not to their relatives, during funerals they abstain from various [traditional] rites, etc. The membership of the Society as well as its treasury are growing. By the beginning of the current year there was $70.20 in the treasury.

For the Russian Christmas (Nativity), the time when Indians engage in heathen celebrations, Brotherhood members decided to organize their own party and invited all the Indians, and even members of the Presbyterian mission in order to set an example of how to spend time properly. The Brotherhood meeting took place in the evening in the parish school building. Brotherhood members themselves decorated the room with flags and greens. Portraits of the Right Reverend Nikolai, Bishop of Alaska and the Aleutians, and Metropolitan Innokentii were prominently displayed and decorated with greens. Tea, bread, and fruit brought by the Brotherhood members were placed on the tables. Guests arrived at 7 p.m., among them were *toions*, Presbyterians, and those who were not Brotherhood members, altogether about 200 people. The meeting was opened with the singing of the holiday hymns "Thy Nativity" ["Rozhdestvo Tvoe"] and "The Virgin Today" ["Deva Dnes' "] performed by the orphanage students together with the Indians. Then everybody sat down to eat. At first it was quiet but then each participant got up and delivered a speech. The first one to rise was a Presbyterian who spoke in his native language and said the following, "Everything here appeals to us—this peaceful meal, the decoration of the room, the order of things, and your society, but most of all we like the close relationship that you have with your pastor [priest]. The white man despises us Indians, even in our mission he disdains us and would not sit at the same table with us; among you, however, the white man and the Indian are all equal in Christ—this touches and moves us."

Another Indian spoke about the darkness of ignorance, where he used to be and where those who did not attend this celebration still remained. "About two years ago I became ill," he began, "the illness was serious. I consulted a shaman [íxt'] who announced that a spirit [yéik] was inside of me and that he would exorcise it. He demanded a payment and I brought him several blankets. The curing took a long time and a lot of goods were given to the shaman, but my sickness only got worse. My relatives advised me to give more to the shaman. I was completely ruined.

One day I decided to go to the [Russian] priest [batiushka]; he treated other Indians, so I thought that he might help me as well. He gave me a jar of medicine. I drank some but began to have some doubts again, thinking that it was useless, since the shaman himself could not help me. Again I brought him a blanket. Again he could not help me. I began getting ready to die. In the evening I decided to drink the priest's medicine, thinking that it would not hurt me anyway. So I pulled myself together and drank it. I did feel better and soon recovered. I was an ignorant man then, and how many of such ignorant people do we still have in the village?" He then continued, "All were invited to come here, but many preferred to participate in their dances and festivities and refused to believe that being here is better . . . . I pray to God that their eyes would be opened as mine have been." Later on Indians also spoke about their former and present life, and other subjects. Their speeches were both expressive and reasonable. Their discussion ended late, about 11 o'clock, when they began to leave.

A similar meeting was organized by the St. Nicholas [Russian] Brotherhood on New Year's Day. To greet the New Year in prayer and with one's family is not a custom of the Russian people of Sitka. The open saloons are a great temptation for the Orthodox population of Alaska. In order to keep the Russians away from that temptation, Fr. Archimandrite Anatolii suggested, during one of the Brotherhood meetings, that the members spend New Year's Eve at a quiet meal. Members of the Brotherhood agreed. The meeting also took place in the parish school building. Members themselves brought tea, bread, and fruit, and invited all the Russians. Altogether about 40 people came.

The meeting began with the singing of the prayer "Heavenly King" ["Tsariu Nebesnyi"] and the hymn in honor of St. Nicholas, the heavenly patron of the Brotherhood. Then all the participants sat down. During the meal the President of the Brotherhood, teacher V. Burov, got up and delivered a speech. In his address to the Brotherhood members he pointed out that their meal reminded one of an evening of brotherly love among the first Christians. He ended his speech by saying "Lately there has been no closeness among Brotherhood members; they are losing interest in the organization, which is the result of mistrust among the members and the lack of their acquaintance with each other. The present meeting is bringing us closer together." Later on the following persons spoke: Fr. Archimandrite Anatolii, Brotherhood secretary Arkhangel'skii, *starosta* [warden] of the St. Michael Cathedral Sergei Kostromitinov, and many other Brotherhood members. Each speech was filled with sincere wishes to have more friendship among Brotherhood members and to work together for the common good. During the meeting the orphanage children sang the Russian anthem and "Many Years" ["Mnogoe Leta"] to the honorable patron of the Brotherhood, the Right Reverend Nikolai, Bishop of Alaska and the Aleutians. The meeting ended at 11 o'clock.

The Christmas-tide is over. Because the holidays were characterized by social rapprochement and reasonable pastime, they will probably be remembered by the entire population of Sitka for a long time.

[*Russian Orthodox American Messenger*, 1897-98, vol. 2, no. 11, pp. 345-8. By S. P-ov (Sergei Popov?)]

Appendix 16

Hieromonk Antonii
Report
on the State of the St. Michael Indian Brotherhood in Sitka
for the year 1902

1902 (the year under review) was the best in the life of the St. Michael Indian Brotherhood; it was a year of true Christian charity and salutary success.

Prior to that the Brotherhood could not boast about either the number of its members or the order within its ranks. Ideas of harmony, Orthodoxy, kind Christian unity would not take root in this institution of the Sitka parish. The cause of this was the inexperience of the leadership and the inaccuracy of the statutes, as well as the fact that the matters of formal protocol completely overshadowed the inner meaning and purpose of this useful church organization.

The past year was characterized by radical regeneration. In order to steer the Brotherhood in the proper direction, several members, who caused disorder in its midst by their excessive claims and demands, had to be sacrificed. However, this quantitative loss was immediately compensated; as soon as this harmful ballast had been removed from the institution, the Brotherhood membership grew from a weak figure of twenty to a respectable one of one hundred and ten. In addition a new healthy spirit could be felt in this new body—a spirit of obedience to the Church and the pastoral leadership, and of strong opposition to false belief.

The most gratifying developments could be mentioned in the following order. In the year under review, Brotherhood members led an exemplary life: there was not a single case of drinking, quarrels, litigation and altercations. The title of a Brotherhood member gained full respect not only among their neighbors in the Sitka Village but in other communities as well. Brotherhood members attended church services willingly and in large numbers; they also tried not to miss the regular weekly services. During holidays, they were present in the church *in corpore* [in person] dressed in uniforms and holding lit candles. The charitable activities of the Brotherhood were so successful that there was no need in the past year to take money out of the main treasury, since each sum needed for mutual aid was immediately covered by a collection.

Relations between members were characterized by peace, friendliness, affability, politeness—all of which made cooperation much easier. Five Brotherhood members were married in church, so as to demonstrate their departure from the primitive naturalized family and strong solidarity with the persistent demands of the Church concerning this subject. Other Brotherhood members decided to submit to these demands as well.

Many members of the Brotherhood announced their desire to learn to read the book of God's Law [the Bible] in their native language. Two of them have demonstrated a complete and rapid success, while others are also on the way to similar achievements in the domain of spiritual enlightenment. Thus this precious book reached their intelligent minds for the first time and immediately became their favorite. Successful education required an alphabet which is now being completed by this author, who has combined the modern methodical system with the phonetic base developed by the deceased Archbishop Innokentii, whose profound observations in this area are extremely useful.

In short, a new spirit and a yearning for spiritual freedom began to glimmer inside the Brotherhood, whereas in the past it was overwhelmed by quarrels, arguments, and other examples of spiritual impoverishment.

During the Christmas [Nativity] holidays Brotherhood members managed to organize an elaborate, wonderful party. The idea of this social innovation belongs entirely to a respected member of the Sitka parish, Brotherhood member Foma [Thomas] Kichkau Bennet, as well as to Nikifor Kul'kita, and their families. The party had been organized according to a special plan, which turned out to be quite successful. After the candles had been lit on the holiday tree, brotherhood members turned to the holy icons and, in full harmony as well as with strength and religious inspiration, sang a *tropar'* and a *kondak* [holiday hymns] in honor of Christ's Nativity. Following that a venerable elderly man delivered a rather eloquent speech. He spoke about a new era in the Indian existence. In accordance with the optimistic ideas of the speech, expensive gifts were distributed among the guests. Many visitors from the distant areas of central Alaska as well as about fifty non-Orthodox Indians were present. They were greatly impressed by the orderly conduct and generosity of the Orthodox Brotherhood members. The most solemn moment of this whole exchange of ideas, holiday wishes, and expressions of sincerity was an eloquent and convincing speech made by Mr. Kichkau Bennet, one of the most high-born Indians. The speaker announced that he was forever abandoning the customs of pagan ignorance and thus decided to part with an ancient crest of his clan. There are only three such regalia among the old as well as the more recent Sitka clans: two historical hats and a staff decorated with human hair and allegoric-heraldic images. This staff was presented to the priest of the Sitka parish. The donor spoke about its historical significance—a combination of a symbol of aristocratic power and hereditary honor of the clan; he also politely asked not to pay special attention to the relative modesty of the gift as a material object but rather to appreciate its special national significance . . . .

The transfer of the above-mentioned artifact in front of such a large group of people had a special outstanding significance; it was also a clear indication of the sympathy and trust between the Church and the Indians. Following that the party continued with an atmosphere of sincerity, mutual friendliness and spiritual unity. This privately initiated attempt to do something good for others is a very important and pleasant fact in the life of the Brotherhood. The fact that Brotherhood members maintained full neutrality in the dangerous local issue of raising and especially "pulling down statues [crests]" does them special credit . . . . While Presbyterian Tlingit all joined a pagan feast that did not fit in with the strict Puritanical morality of their religion, the Orthodox Brotherhood members behaved very well; having rejected the appeal to join the ceremony, they peacefully conducted their family affairs, attended the church and religious meetings, and could not be seduced by the loud noises made by the participants in the feast, or by the food and drink available there. This is one more wonderful indication of the wisdom and prudence of the Brotherhood members who were able to resist the superstitions and violence of their tribal kin.

Another pleasant fact of equal importance should also be mentioned. Some time ago the Sitka Brotherhood resisted and destroyed all the attempts of the local branch of the Salvation Army (using this new cover to promote Presbyterian interests) to subvert them. Because of that the street prophets rushed to the most distant and backward Tlingit settlements. The most energetic forces of the Army went to Killisnoo. Incidentally, our own young psalm-reader left his post there just before the Christmas-tide. The needs of the local church were tremendous. A preacher, a translator, and a constant helper in those difficult times was greatly needed. The Sitka Brotherhood immediately realized the danger posed by this cunning redecorated enemy. Brotherhood member Semeon Kakoish [Luke Semean] asked my advice whether he should go there to talk to the people about not losing their heads and remaining loyal to Orthodoxy. Although it was difficult for me to give an official permission, I gladly blessed the good Brotherhood member, supplied him with Orthodox instructional materials in the Indian [Tlingit] and English languages, and sent him off for further instructions to the priest of the Killisnoo parish. This turned out to be a timely and very helpful measure. Semeon Kakoish [Luke Semean] attracted eighty-three members to the Orthodox Brotherhood, stopped the people from being carried away from our Church by the street preachers, and was quite successful in making them listen to him. The voice of a tranquil, dedicated, and wise man overcame the street shouting of the disguised Presbyterians. Local people trusted their brother and left his adversaries. Since then the false prophets of Killisnoo have suffered a serious decline, the usual thing in these situations . . . .

[*Russian Orthodox American Messenger*, vol. 7, no. 4, 1903, pp. 56-60.]

TLINGIT GLOSSARY

aankáawu	chief, headman, rich man
aatlein aankáawu	senior chief, head chief
ch'áak'	eagle
(kaa) daakeidí	mortuary pole, grave house, grave, coffin
dagankú	land of the dead
dzísk'w	moose
(ax) éesh	(my) father
ganook	petrel
gooch	wolf
guneitkanaayí	people of the opposite moiety
góos'	cloud cover, cloudy sky
Gus'k'iyeekwáan	Europeans, whites; lit. "people from under (i.e., supporting) the base of the clouds"
gus'yadóoli	sandpiper
guwakaan	deer
íxt'	shaman, medicine man
káa	human being, man
(ax) káani	(my) brother-in-law or sister-in-law
kéet	killer whale
keewakáawu	celestial realm (of the dead), literally means "man" or "lord of keewa.áa'
kóon	flicker
kóoshdaa	land otter
kootéeyaa	totem pole
láx'	heron
lingít	Tlingit, person
lóol	fireweed
l'ook	coho (silver) salmon
naaxein	Chilkat blanket
nakws'aatí	witch

149

saak	eulachen (candlefish)
sáanáx̱	south or southwest wind
(ax̱) sáni	(my) father's brother
s'áaxw	ceremonial hat
sheishóox̱	rattle
xeitl	thunderbird
xíxch'	frog
(ax̱) x̱ooní	(my) tribesman, friend
x̱óots	brown bear
yaakw	canoe
yéik	shaman's spirit (helper) yéik can be singular or plural; yéikx' is specifically a collective plural, "(a group of) spirits"
yéil	raven
wootsaagáa	ceremonial staff

RUSSIAN GLOSSARY

amanatstvo	taking of hostages (from 'amanat'—hostage)
arshin	Russian linear measure, 28 inches
barabora (borabora, barabara)	usually refers to a small semi-permanent dwelling or shelter, or any semi-subterranean dwelling of native Siberians or Alaskans; in the nineteenth century applied to permanent wooden native dwellings, including the Tlingit winter house
bobr	beaver; sea otter, cf. *morskoi bobr*
chaga	Sitka spruce
iamanina	goat meat
iukola	dried fish
kaftan	caftan (long tunic with a waist girdle)
kalga	slave (of native Alaskans)
kiziuch	coho (silver) salmon
Kolchane (Gol'tsane)	Kolchan. (Athabaskans of the Interior—Upper Copper River, Upper Kuskokwim, and Upper Innoko)
Kolosh (Kaliuzh, Koliuzh)	Russian term for the Tlingit
koriushka	smelt
kuiak	armor (old Russian)
laida	tide flat
lopushnik (lapushnik)	burdock (*Arctium lappa* or *Lappa major*)
Mednovtsy	Lower Ahtna and sometimes Eyak
moroshka	cloudberry (*Rubus chamaemorus*)
morskoi kot	fur seal
nerpa	seal
nezamainik	devilclub (*Oplopanax horridus*)
promyshlennik	hunter, fur trapper, fur trader, entrepreneur

151

sazhen'	Russian linear measure, 7 feet
shiksha	crowberry (*Empetrum nigrum*)
shishak	helmet
sivuch	sea lion
taion (toion, toen)	chief (among native Siberians and Alaskans, probably of Yakut origin)
Ugalentsy (Ugaliakhmiuty)	Eyak
uril (uril morskoi)	cormorant
versta	Russian linear measure, 3500 feet
vydra	otter

BIBLIOGRAPHY

I. *Books and Articles*

Afonsky, Gregory, Bishop
1977   *A History of the Orthodox Church in Alaska.* Kodiak, Alaska: St. Herman's Theological Seminary.

Averkieva, Iuliia P.
1960   K istorii obshchestvennogo stroia u indeitsev severozapadnogo poberezh'ia Severnoi Ameriki [On the History of the Social Order of the Indians of the Northwest Coast of North America]. *Trudy Instituta Etnografii im. N.N. Miklukho-Maklaia*, n.s., vol. 58:5-126.

Black, Lydia
1977   The Konyag (The Inhabitants of the Island of Kodiak) by Iosaf (Bolotov) (1794-1799) and by Gideon (1804-1807). *Arctic Anthropology* 14(2):79-108.

Dauenhauer, Nora, and Dauenhauer, Richard L.
1976   *Beginning Tlingit.* Anchorage, Alaska: Tlingit Readers, Inc.

Dauenhauer, Richard L.
1975   *Text and Context in the Tlingit Oral Tradition.* Unpublished Ph.D. Dissertation in Comparative Literature, University of Wisconsin, Madison.

de Laguna, Frederica
1960   The Story of a Tlingit Community. *Bureau of American Ethnology Bulletin* 172. Washington, D.C.: U.S. Government Printing Office.

1972   *Under Mount Saint Elias: The History and Culture of the Yakutat Tlingit.* Vols. 1-3. Washington, D.C.: Smithsonian Institution Press.

Documents Relative to the History of Alaska
1936-38 Unpublished manuscript. University of Alaska, Fairbanks.

Donskoi, Vladimir, Fr.
1893   Sitkha i Koloshi [Sitka and the Tlingit]. *Tserkovnye Vedomosti* 22:822-828; 23:856-862.

1895   *Molitvy na Koloshenskom Narechii* [Prayers in the Tlingit Language]. Sitka, Alaska: n.p.

Drucker, Philip
  1958   The Native Brotherhoods: Modern Intertribal Organizations on
          the Northwest Coast. *Bureau of American Ethnology Bulletin* 168.
          Washington, D.C.: U.S. Printing Office.

Emmons, George T.
  1911   An Account of the Meeting between La Perouse and the Tlingit.
          American Anthropologist, n.s., 13:294-298.

  n.d.   The Tlingit Indians. Unpublished manuscript. Archives, American
          Museum of Natural History, New York.

Freeze, Gregory L.
  1983   *The Parish Clergy in Nineteenth-century Russia.* Princeton, New
          Jersey: Princeton University Press.

Glass, Henry
  1890   Naval Administration in Alaska. *The Proceedings of the United
          States Naval Institute*, vol. XVI, no. 1, whole no. 52:1-19.

Gunther, Erna
  1972   *Indian Life on the Northwest Coast of North America.* Chicago:
          University of Chicago Press.

Hallock, Charles
  1902   The Ancestors of the American Indigenes. *American Antiquarian*
          24(1):3-18.

Hinckley, Ted C.
  1972   *The Americanization of Alaska, 1867-1897.* Palo Alto, California:
          Pacific Books Publishers.

  1982   *Alaskan John G. Brady, Missionary, Businessman, Judge, and
          Governor, 1878-1918.* Columbus, Ohio: Ohio State University
          Press.

Holmberg, Heinrich J.
  1856   Ethnographische Skizzen uber die Volker des Russischen Amerika.
          Acta Societatis Scientiarum Fennicae 4:281-421. Helsinki.

  1985   *Holmberg on Russian America*, edited by Marvin Falk and translated
          by Fritz Jaensch. Rasmuson Library Translation Series Vol. I,
          Fairbanks: University of Alaska Press.

Jones, Livingstone F.
  1914   *A Study of the Thlingets of Alaska.* New York: Fleming H. Revell
          Co.

Kamenskii, Anatolii, Archimandrite

1899   *Indianskoe Plemia Tlingit* [The Tlingit Indians]. New York: Russian
Orthodox American Messenger.

1908   *Amerikanskie Ocherki* [American Sketches]. Odessa: Fesenko
Publishing House.

Kan, Sergei

1979-   Ethnographic fieldnotes from 13 Months' Fieldwork
1980   among the Tlingit of Southeastern Alaska. (Manuscript in Kan's
possession.)

1982   *Wrap Your Father's Brothers in Kind Words: an Analysis of the
Nineteenth-century Tlingit Mortuary and Memorial Rituals.*
Unpublished Ph.D. Dissertation in Anthropology, University of
Chicago.

1983   Russian Orthodox Missionaries and the Tlingit Indians of Alaska,
1880-1900. Paper presented at the Second Laurier Conference on
North American Ethnohistory and Ethnology, Huron College,
University of Western Ontario. London, Ontario, Canada.

1984   Russian Orthodox Brotherhoods among the Tlingit Indians:
Missionary Goals and Native Response. (To be published in
Ethnohistory.)

Khlebnikov, Kyrill T.

1973   *Baranov, Chief Manager of the Russian Colonies in America.*
Kingston, Ontario: The Limestone Press. [Originally published in
Russian in 1835.]

Knapp, Frances, and Childe, Rheta L.

1896   *The Thlinkets of Southeastern Alaska.* Chicago: Stone and Kimball.

Krause, Aurel

1970   *The Tlingit Indians.* Translated by Erna Gunther. Seattle: University
of Washington Press. [Originally published in German in 1885].

Lisianskii, Iurii

1947   *Puteshestvie vokrug sveta na korable "Neva," v 1803-1806 gg.* [A
Journey around the World Aboard the *Neva*, 1803-1806]. Moscow:
OGIZ. [Originally published in 1812.]

Litke, Fedor P.
 1948 *Puteshestvie vokrug sveta na voennom shliupe "Seniavin" v 1826-1829*
    gg. [A Journey around the World Aboard the Military Ship
    Seniavin, 1826-1829.] 2 ed. Moscow: OGIZ. [Originally published
    in 1834.]

McClellan, Catharine
 1954 The Interrelation of Social Structure with Northern Tlingit
    Ceremonialism. *Southwestern Journal of Anthropology* 10:75-96.

 1970 The Girl who Married the Bear: a Masterpiece of Indian Oral
    Tradition. *National Museum of Man. Publications in Ethnology* 2.
    Ottawa, Canada.

Meletinskii, Eleazar M.
 1979 *Paleoaziatskii Mifologicheskii Epos. Tsikl Vorona* [The Paleoasian
    Mythological Epos. The Raven Cycle]. Moscow: Nauka.

Morgan, Lewis H.
 1877 *Ancient Society.* New York: Holt.

Nadezhdin, Ivan
 1896 *Sbornik tserkovnykh pesnopenii i molitvoslovii na koloshenskom narechii*
    [A Collection of Church Hymns and Prayers in the Tlingit
    Language]. San Francisco: n.p.

Oberg, Kalervo
 1937 *The Social Economy of the Tlingit Indians.* Unpublished Ph.D.
    Dissertation in Anthropology, University of Chicago.

Olson, Ronald
 1967 Social Structure and Social Life of the Tlingit Indians in Alaska.
    University of California Anthropological Records 26.

Pierce, Richard (ed.)
 1978 *The Russian Orthodox Religious Mission in America, 1794-1837.*
    Kingston, Ontario: The Limestone Press. [Originally published in
    Russian in 1894.]

 1980 *The Journals of Iakov Netsvetov: the Atkha Years, 1828-1844.*
    Translated from Russian by Lydia Black. Kingston, Ontario: The
    Limestone Press.

Rasmussen, Knud
 1938 Knud Rasmussen's Posthumous Notes on the Life and Doings of
    the East Greenlanders in Olden Times. Edited by H. Ostermann.
    Meddelelser om Grønland, bd. 109, Nr. 1.

Ratner-Shternberg, S.A.
1930 Muzeinye materialy po tlingitam. Ocherk III [Museum Collection of Tlingit Artifacts. Part III]. *Sbornik Muzeia Antropologii i Etnografii*, vol. 9:167-186.

Shotridge, Louis
1917 My Northland Revisited. *Museum Journal* 8:105-115.

1928 The Emblems of the Tlingit Culture. *Museum Journal* 19:350-377.

1929 The Bride of Tongass. A Study of the Tlingit Marriage Ceremony. *Museum Journal* 29:131-156.

Smith, Barbara S.
1980 *Russian Orthodoxy in Alaska*. Alaska Historical Commission: [Anchorage].

Solov'ev, Vladimir S.
1901- *Sobranie Sochinenii*, [Collected Works], 9 vols. St. Petersburg.
1907

Swanton, John R.
1908 Social Conditions, Beliefs, and Linguistic Relationships of the Tlingit Indians. In *26th Annual Report of the Bureau of American Ethnology*. Washington, D.C.: U.S. Government Printing Office. Pp. 391-486.

1909 Tlingit Myths and Texts. *Bureau of American Ethnology Bulletin* 39. Washington, D.C.: U.S. Government Printing Office.

Tarasar, Constance (ed.)
1975 *Orthodox America, 1794-1976*. Syosset, New York: The Orthodox Church in America.

Tikhmenev, Petr A.
1978 *A History of the Russian-American Company*. Seattle: University of Washington Press. [Originally published in Russian in 1861-1863.]

Tokarev, Sergei A.
1957 *Religioznye verovaniia vostochnoslavianskikh narodov XIX-nachala XX vekov* [Religious Beliefs of the Eastern Slavs in the 19th-early 20th centuries]. Moscow: Nauka.

Townsend, Joan B.
1981 Tanaina. In *Handbook of North American Indians. Vol. 6, Subarctic*. June Helm (ed.). Washington, D.C.: Smithsonian Institution. Pp. 623-640.

VanStone, James W.
   1967   *Eskimos of the Nushagak River*. Seattle: University of Washington Press.

Vdovin, I.S. (ed.)
   1979   *Khristianstvo i lamaism u korennogo naseleniia Sibiri* [Christianity and Lamaism among the Aboriginal Population of Siberia]. Leningrad: Nauka.

Veniaminov, Ivan
   1840   *Zapiski ob ostrovakh Unalashkinskogo Otdela* [Notes on the Islands of the Unalaska District]. St. Petersburg: Synodal Press.

   1846   *Zamechaniia o koloshenskom i kadiakskom iazykakh* [Notes on the Tlingit and the Kodiak Languages]. St. Petersburg: Imperial Academy of Science.

   1886   *Tvoreniia* [Collected Works]. Vols. 1-3. Edited by Ivan Barsukov. Moscow: Synodal Press.

   1984   *Notes on the Islands of the Unalaska District*. Translated by Lydia T. Black and R. H. Geoghegan, edited by Richard A. Pierce. Kingston, Ontario: Elmer E. Rasmuson Library Translation Program and The Limestone Press.

Wilbur, Bertrand K.
   n.d.   *Just About Me—Medical Missionary to Sitka, 1894-1901*. Unpublished Manuscript, Sitka Historical Society, Sitka, Alaska.

Zuboff, Robert (Shaadaax')
   1973   *Kudatan Kahidée* (The Salmon Box). Sitka, Alaska: Tlingit Readers, Inc./Sheldon Jackson College.

II. *Periodicals*

The Alaskan, 1885-1907
The Assembly Herald, 1908-1914
Home Mission Monthly, 1915-1923
North Star, 1889-1898
Russian Orthodox American Messenger, 1896-1939
Thlinget, 1908-1912
Verstovian, 1914-1972

III. *Manuscript Collections*

Juneau, Alaska. Archives of St. Nicholas Russian Orthodox Church. Records of the Juneau and Killisnoo Parishes, 1894-1911.

Sitka, Alaska. Archives. Stratton Memorial Library, Sheldon Jackson College.

Sitka, Alaska. Archives of the Diocese of Alaska, Orthodox Church in America. Records of the Sitka and Other Parishes of Southeastern Alaska, 1866-1917.

Washington, D.C. Library of Congress. Manuscript Division. The Alaska Russian Church Collection.

INDEX